C000142060

Loved by fans because they love the fans

BILL Shankly once remarked: "I'm just one of the people who stands on the Kop. They think the same as I do and I think the same as they do. It's a kind of marriage of people who like each other."

The great Scot was speaking of his love affair with the Liverpool crowd and the almost spiritual connection reciprocated between the followers in the stand and their charismatic messiah.

Shanks made the comment more than 30 years ago and so it is a tribute to Jamie Carragher's status at the club that those words could easily have been attributed to the defensive rock currently plying his trade at Anfield and who this official tribute edition is dedicated to.

The Bootle-born defender has a natural affinity with the club's supporters and a passion and commitment to Liverpool Football Club that would have made Shankly proud.

Ask your average Kopite who they think Liverpool's most inspirational player of recent times is and they may well pick out Steven Gerrard.

But ask them who represents the fan on the street when they pull on the famous red shirt and most will not hesitate to say 'Carra'.

Under Rafa Benitez he has grown into the mainstay at the heart of the Reds' defence, sweating blood for the cause and running through the proverbial brick wall to ensure Liverpool succeed.

But it is not just Carra's no-nonsense style and heart-on-the-sleeve mentality that was so apparent during the club's heroic Champions League campaign in 2005 that has seen him earn his well-deserved place among Liverpool's elite.

It is also his humility and commitment to his scouse roots.

Ten years on from his first-team debut he has evolved from being Liverpool's Mr Versatile into our Mr Dependable, racking up over 400 appearances.

The path to becoming one of Europe's best defenders has been littered with countless diversions but after years of fighting off the competition in both the full-back positions he has finally started to receive the recognition he deserves.

From an FA Youth Cup triumph as a holding midfielder in 1996 through to his heroics at the back in Istanbul, Carragher has emerged into one of the most respected centre-halves in the Premiership.

United by passion

CARRA

Jamie Carragher talks exclusively to PAUL HASSALL about the highs and lows of 10 years at Liverpool Football Club

FROM his first taste of success in the 1996 Youth Cup final through to the glory of winning the FA Cup for the second time in 2006, Jamie Carragher has experienced some extraordinary highs in over a decade at English football's most successful club.

And yet as we sit down to reminisce about his time at Anfield, there is an air of bewilderment that surrounds him.

"92 pages all on me?"

His expression is one of shock.

"On me?" he asks again before shaking his head in disbelief.

His surprise is genuine and is his reaction to the news that he is set to feature in a special publication chronicling the 10 years since he made his debut for the Reds in the League Cup on January 8, 1997.

It is typical of the man – unassuming yet endearing.

He is an England international who has played in the World Cup finals and made over 400 appearances for Liverpool, and yet he remains as modest as the youngster who grew up playing the game he loves for the sheer joy of it.

It was there, in the Marsh Lane area of Bootle, that the young Carra began his football odyssey.

His talent was evident early on and in his early teens he signed as an apprentice with Liverpool Football Club.

But it would not be until years later, on a cold January night down by the Riverside, that he would take his first major step towards becoming an Anfield legend.

His big moment came in the 75th minute of a fourth round Coca-Cola Cup tie with Middlesbrough when he replaced regular right-back Rob Jones.

The Reds went on to lose the match that night but it is a memory that will remain with Carra for the rest of his life and one that he remembers vividly.

"To be honest I thought I was going to start the game," he says, his mind wandering back to that momentous occasion.

"But the boss (Roy Evans) picked Rob Jones instead. It was his first game back after an injury, so I ended up coming on as sub.

"We lost 2-1 and I probably had a good chance to score. I hit a decent shot but Robbie (Fowler) got in the way. I thought it was going in.

"I remember that John Barnes didn't play in that game. He was getting a bit of criticism at the time, but I think that probably told everyone that he was a big part of the team because it was obvious to see that we missed him."

Having enjoyed his first taste of action alongside the likes of Robbie Fowler, Steve McManaman and Patrik Berger at the Riverside, Carra was eager for more and just 10 days later he was marking his first start for the club with a goal in front of the Kop.

"I remember Stig (Bjornebye) took an outswinging corner and I just got free and flicked it in," he says.

"They had no-one on the post, Bosnich was in goal and I was probably free because it was my first game and no-one really knew who I was.

"Gerard Houllier had a big influence on my career just because of the age I was when he came in. I used to hang on his every word."

"We went on to win 3-0 and we were top of the league that night, so it was a great day for me."

While the match was to signal the end of Carra's brief flirtation with the limelight for that season, he had done enough to convince both himself and the manager that he could play a big part in Liverpool's future.

Reflecting upon his feelings at the time, Carra admits that he never imagined that he would be the solitary figure – apart from the returning Robbie Fowler – from that side to still be playing at the club today.

"It's nice to have been around so long but I don't think you ever look too far ahead," he says . "Especially when you first get into the team.

"You maybe look after yourself a bit more and try to get involved in as many games as possible.

"I was a midfielder back then and the club went and bought Paul Ince as well so obviously I thought it would take a bit of time to establish myself.

"But it actually came about pretty quickly and I got into the side at about 19 the following season, and started playing in different defensive positions.

"There's been a lot of times when the manager brought different players in, that people thought maybe I wouldn't play as much or that I wouldn't have been here much longer.

"But obviously it has all worked out and I'm delighted to have been here, at a club like Liverpool, for this long."

The team has undergone a series of dramatic transformations since those early days but despite working under three managers with contrasting views on the game, Carragher has remained an integral part of first team plans throughout.

Looking back on each manager's tenure at the club, Carra offers an interesting insight into just how different they were.

"Roy (Evans) was obviously the one who gave me my chance," he says fondly.

"He was great and just like one of the

lads really. You realised the history he had at the club and the experience he had from working with people like Bill Shankly. You can't help but learn from that.

"But then Gerard Houllier came in and changed things around. His ways were a lot stricter and there was a lot more discipline about the place then.

"He had a very big influence on my career just because of the age I was when he came in. I was about 20, 21. I used to hang on his every word because at that age you take everything in.

"Then there's Rafa (Benitez) and again he's a bit different.

"Whereas Gerard Houllier was concerned with both football and off the field activities, I think Rafa is more football, football, football.

"Obviously he wants you to live your life right but he isn't as big on that as maybe Houllier was."

From Roy Evans'

"Playing football with John Barnes every day was special. He had skills and ability that I've not seen anyone else with."

side of attack-minded possession football and Gerard Houllier's counter-attacking treble winners through to the heights of Rafa Benitez's tactically sound European champions, Carra's influence on the side has continued to increase as he has matured into one of the best defenders in the Premiership.

But while he credits all three managers for their contribution to his development he has no doubts as to who has had the biggest impact on his career.

"From a professional point of view it would have to be Rafa Benitez," he says.

"I won the European Cup under him and I've definitely learnt a lot from the manager in the past three seasons – especially from the

football and tactical side of it.

"Off the field I'd have to say my dad because he's been there since I first started playing as a kid."

One of the overriding factors behind Carra's 10-year stay at Anfield has been each manager's faith in not only his undoubted ability, but his infectious personality and unquestionable commitment.

For many he is the perfect example of what characteristics are required in order to wear the famous red shirt and with this in mind, you can see why he has seen so many people come and go during that time.

But out of all the top names to have featured alongside Carra over the years, who does he single out as the best he has ever played with?

"I'd have to pick two," he says.

"John Barnes and Steven Gerrard.

"Obviously Stevie speaks for himself but playing football with John Barnes every day was special. He had skills and ability that I've still not seen anyone else with to this day.

"He's the best finisher I've ever seen and you may think that's strange because I've played with Michael Owen and Robbie Fowler," he says with the enthusiasm of a fan.

"But his goals and his finishing in training... ▶

Carra credits his dad with being a huge influence on his career

▶ "He used to do things that you couldn't believe. I mean, I never saw him give the ball away. Two-footed and strong, he was just an outstanding player."

Few would argue with his choice.

Indeed had the modern day Liverpool been able to call upon the flair of a player like John Barnes in his prime then who knows how close they could have come to recapturing the all-conquering glory of days gone by?

But that's not to undermine the success the Reds have achieved recently.

Carra has still enjoyed more than his fair share of trophy successes as a Liverpool player.

The first cup win came in 2001 with that historic treble, a season that was both exhausting and exhilarating.

"Winning the treble was something unbelievable when you actually think

"Istanbul will probably go down as one of the greatest games ever. It was like a film. You went from one extreme to the other with how you felt at half-time to how you felt at the end."

about it," he says.

"Three trophies in one season was a great achievement, especially as towards the end of it the games were coming thick and fast.

"But the thing about Gerard Houllier was that although he changed the team around, he never changed the back four so it was just Babbel, Hyypia, Henchoz and me every game.

"I think we had a spell where we played five or six games in something like 11 days.

"We played so many games it was unbelievable.

"I think it told in the UEFA Cup final and even in the FA Cup final really because we weren't our normal selves.

"But with the UEFA Cup final, even though it was a great game, it shouldn't have got to that.

"We were far too good for Alaves. You could see that at the start of the game.

"Our legs had gone towards the end of the season but we just hung on in there."

And yet for all the high points of the treble-winning season, when you ask Carra what his greatest memory in a Reds shirt is, he has no hesitation in choosing one match that even surpassed the achievements of the class of 2001.

"It's got to be Istanbul," he says, the occasion still evoking an unmistakable

twinkle in his eyes.

"Even if we go on and win the Champions League again, I don't think it will ever beat that. It was the way we won it more than anything.

"I think that will probably go down as one of the greatest games ever ... I mean I can't think of many better games in the history of football, can you?

"It was like a film. You went from one

extreme to the other with how you felt at half-time to how you felt at the end of the game.

"Didi coming on at half-time, Jerzy's save, my cramp and Stevie changing position and having a great game – so many things happened.

"Everyone's got their own story about where they were, how they watched it, how they were at half-time, what they did at the end of the game. It's like everyone's played a part in it.

"It's something that will stay with us forever."

The road to the Ataturk proved to be almost as eventful as the final itself with the story of the club's most memorable European nights being re-written with each passing round.

For drama see Olympiakos.

For raw passion and emotion see Juventus.

But for sheer power and volume you-just had to witness Chelsea part two.

Carragher remembers the semi-final second leg against Jose Mourinho's men vividly and admits he has never experienced an atmosphere at Anfield quite like it.

"It was an amazing night," he recalls.

"We got the early goal which Chelsea are still crying about but let's face it, it should have been a penalty and a red card.

"If you'd offered me that or the goal

board, the crowd carried us across the line."

Listening to Carragher re-live some of his finest moments in a Liverpool shirt makes you realise just how much he has achieved during his time with the Reds. He has played in some of the greatest matches in living memory and although the Premiership title continues to elude him, he insists that the past decade has been a wonderful time to be a Red.

Sami Hyypia and Stephane Henchoz were the backbone of the 2001 defence

My top five games

1) 'Istanbul. I don't need to say anything else really, do I?'

2) 'I think I'd have to say when we won the FA Cup for the first time (2001 v Arsenal). We were never in it really but Michael got those two goals and it was just a great feeling.'

3) 'The second leg against Chelsea in the semi-final of the Champions League (2005). It was probably my best game for Liverpool. We were under the cosh but the atmosphere at Anfield was unbelievable.'

4) 'The Goodison derby (3-2 v Everton, 2001) when Gary McAllister scored in the last minute. That was an amazing game and it put us well on the way to achieving Champions League football for the next season.

'I'd love to score against Everton, especially at Goodison Park. I wish I'd scored that free-kick that day – it would have been great.'

5) 'I've been very lucky because I've played in some great cup finals and the match against Alaves was probably the greatest UEFA Cup final of all-time. It was a rollercoaster of a match but we deserved to win it.'

I'd have taken the keeper getting sent off and the penalty.

"But anyway, we went on and it was probably one of the greatest ever atmospheres at Anfield.

"It's up there with Inter Milan and St Etienne in years gone by.

"I think the six minutes of added on time is what wound everyone up, but although a few of the lads were a little bit deflated when they saw it on the

"The 60s, 70s, and 80s for Liverpool were great," says Carra.

"The 90s wasn't the best, but no-one can say that about this decade.

"The trophies we have won have been amazing but it's not just the cups. Some of the games we've played in have been up there with the best games of all time.

"Definitely the best Champions League final, and maybe one of the ▶

▶ best European Cup finals of all-time.

"We've played in the best UEFA Cup final of all time and there's also the FA Cup against West Ham last season. That will go down as one of the best too.

"So we've definitely given value for money to our supporters this decade and with a few years still left of it, hopefully there will be more trophies to come."

Having accomplished so much this millennium, Carra is not short of a medal or two.

But despite boasting a fine display of silverware on his mantelpiece he is desperate to add one more medal in particular to his collection.

"I'd love to have won the league at some point in the last 10 years," he says, the frustration evident in his face.

"I think about it a lot. I probably think about it every day.

"But I suppose that in football you always feel that no matter what you do, there's always someone who has done more than you, so even if we did win the title, I'd want to win it again and again."

The determination in Carragher's face when it comes to talking about winning the title illustrates just how much he wants to end what is now a 17-year wait since the Reds were last crowned champions.

But he is not alone when it comes to the unquenchable thirst that has now become our holy grail.

"It's something we'd love on our CVs and it's probably the only one missing for a few of us, like Sami, myself and Stevie," he says.

"We've probably challenged a couple of times and that's about it, which is not enough.

"We've won virtually everything else really. We missed out on the World Club Championship, which would have been nice, but there's no doubting we've won a lot.

"Hopefully between now and the end of my Liverpool career we'll be challenging for the title a lot more and hopefully we can win it one day."

For a player who has achieved so much in the past six years it would be easy to assume that the bad memories have been few and far between.

But not for Carragher.

When asked what the worst period has been from his ten years in the first team, he is quick to point out that there is no one moment that stands out in his mind.

Instead his choice is simple.

"Losing matches," he says with a grimace that suggests the mere thought of defeat upsets him.

"Bad games always stick in your mind. The mistake I made against Everton this season (3-0 defeat at Goodison Park) still annoys me.

Among Carra's worst memories are the derby defeat in 2006 and the two own goals he scored against Manchester United in 1999

Carra closes down a shot from Ivan Alonso of Alaves in a game the Reds defender describes as 'the best UEFA Cup final of all time'

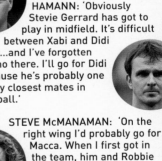

"I remember scoring two own goals against Manchester United in one game too. Bad performances like that annoy me more than anything."

That kind of winning mentality and passion to do well for the club is exactly what has immortalised him as a fans' favourite.

Blue blood may have once pumped through his veins but there is no doubt that he is now a fully converted Red and has become a kindred spirit with those that sing his name in the stands.

"The fans do mean a lot to me," he says.

"I'm a football fan myself, so I know what it's like to stand on the terraces even though it was across the park!

"But I feel like I understand where they are coming from and so to have a good relationship with them is great because it shows they appreciate what you do on the pitch.

"Hopefully they see a little bit of themselves in me because that's what I want them to see."

The type of adoration Carragher enjoys is not something that has happened overnight.

Years of hard work on the training ground have seen him emerge from a utility player with no position to call his own into one of the best home grown youngsters to have ever made it into the Liverpool first team.

So just how far does the man himself think he has come since that January night back in 1997?

"I think I've probably improved all aspects of my game really," he admits.

"I was never like a Steven Gerrard when I first got in the team but I was obviously a good player or I wouldn't have been playing for Liverpool at 19. But people like him and Michael Owen were not far off world class players when they first got in the team.

"I've had to build it up through improvement and experience and that type of thing. But I think I've done that and I'm pleased with how I've progressed. I want to learn and I always work hard and do as ▶

My best Liverpool XI from last 10 years

PEPE REINA: 'I'd have to put Pepe in goal.'

MARKUS BABBEL: 'Babbel or Finnan is a tough one actually. I'll probably go for Markus Babbel at right-back. You can't choose between him and Finn as players but I think Babbel had more chance of getting a goal and I think he got six or seven in the treble season.'

JAMIE CARRAGHER: 'Should I put myself at left-back? John Arne Riise will start crying if I don't put him in. Oh go on, I'll put myself in the team!'

SAMI HYYPIA & STEPHANE HENCHOZ: 'I'll put Sami and Stephane in together at centre-back. I won't put myself in there. That was a great partnership at the time and we won the treble with those two there.

'Sami's still here now and he's still going strong while Stephane would die for you on the pitch. He'd block anything.'

STEVEN GERRARD & DIDI HAMANN: 'Obviously Stevie Gerrard has got to play in midfield. It's difficult between Xabi and Didi then...and I've forgotten Momo there. I'll go for Didi because he's probably one of my closest mates in football.'

STEVE McMANAMAN: 'On the right wing I'd probably go for Macca. When I first got in the team, him and Robbie were the two main men and he carried Liverpool for a few years and went on to win lots of trophies with Real Madrid and had a great career. It's good to get another Scouser in too.'

JOHN BARNES: 'On the left I'd have to have John Barnes. Even though he played central midfield when I got into the team, in his day he was probably one of the best players in the world.'

MICHAEL OWEN & ROBBIE FOWLER: 'I'd have to go for Michael and Robbie up front. Just look at their records.'

Carra in the thick of celebrations after the Reds beat Manchester United in the 2001 Charity Shield at the Millennium Stadium

well as I can in every game and every training session and hopefully it's paid dividends."

Ten trophies and over 400 appearances for the club suggest it has.

The landmark of a decade in the first team at a club of Liverpool's stature is testament to just how important Jamie Carragher has been to the Reds during that time.

Many of the club's greatest names cannot boast such longevity and it is this type of service to a club he holds so dear to his heart that will see him take his much deserved place among Liverpool's illustrious list of legends.

But while 10 years was once an indication that a player's career was coming to an end, Carra is optimistic that there are still a number of chapters in his Liverpool career still to

be written beyond his latest landmark.

"I've still got a few years left in me and hopefully I'll be lucky enough to finish my career at Liverpool," he says.

"Obviously the club comes first and they've got to have the best players on the pitch but hopefully I can keep to a good standard and finish here because I don't really want to play for anyone else."

The day when he finally hangs up his boots may not be for some time yet, but while Carra's Liverpool career is far from in its twilight, the entertaining journey through his memories of L4 has come to an end.

A handshake follows and as he wanders off into the distance I can see he is still shaking his head and muttering to himself.

"92 pages all on me..."

Best opponent I've ever faced: Thierry Henry

I'd have to say him, just for his sheer pace.

'You play against quick players but he's on another level.

'He's turbo charged. When he wants to

turn and go, he can go and he's caused me a few problems down the years.

'But then again (laughs) he's caused everyone problems!'

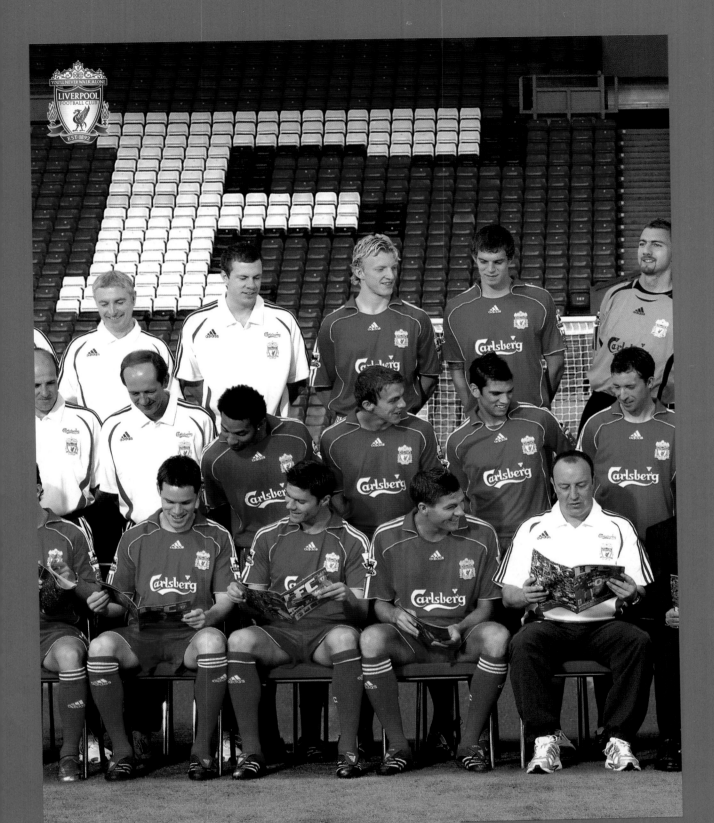

ARE YOU WELL RED?

DON'T MISS LFC MAGAZINE EVERY TUESDAY

SUBSCRIPTIONS HOTLINE: 0845 143 0001

LFC

OFFICIAL MAGAZINE

The early

Carra with his swimming club (third from right, top row), getting treatment before a big game in his junior football days and in his Everton

Young striker who walked away from Liverpool, but changed his mind soon after

IT may be hard to believe now but Jamie Carragher was once a free-scoring striker who went by the nickname of "Sharpy."

The humorous tag was given to him by none other than legendary forward and Liverpool boss at the time, Kenny Dalglish.

It all came about when Carra did the unthinkable and swapped Liverpool's centre of excellence for his boyhood heroes, Everton, in 1988.

It was a moment of madness that was to last just two weeks but on his return to Liverpool, Dalglish began to refer to him as 'Sharpy' after the Everton number nine Graeme Sharp.

"Kenny used to call me Sharpy because I was an Everton fan when I was a kid and I was a striker when I first joined Liverpool," explains Carra.

"I know it's bad isn't it, but that's how

RRA Years

top at school (middle row) before pledging his allegiance to the Reds

I was brought up back then!"

While no-one could doubt Carragher's commitment to the cause nowadays, at the time, the lure of playing at Goodison Park turned his head.

However, Everton proved to be a disappointment to him and the opportunity to see the likes John Barnes, Jan Molby and Kenny Dalglish every day inspired a change of heart.

"I couldn't believe it because Kenny Dalglish actually used to come and watch us train! I mean he was the Liverpool manager and he used to come and watch a bunch of kids train on a week night," says Carra with a sound of disbelief still heard in his voice today.

"I think it was because his son Paul used to train with us then too, but it was still great!

"He would come from Anfield in his suit and watch us train in a local gymnasium at seven or eight o'clock at night which shows how dedicated he was to Liverpool Football Club at that time."

Carra's path to becoming a Liverpool legend began as a six-year-old with his local junior side Merton Villa, where he featured in a position that may ►

Carra by the famous 'This is Anfield' sign before playing there for Bootle Boys, and (above) with a team-mate

Carra enjoys the taste of lifting a trophy at Anfield for the first time after playing in a schools final with Bootle Boys

shock those of you who have grown accustomed to his no-nonsense style of play.

"My first ever position playing football was right or left midfield because I was a lot younger than the other kids," he reveals.

"I was probably six or seven playing under-10s football for Villa so I think they tried to keep me out of the middle really, where it is a bit more physical."

The St James' Primary School pupil made an instant impression and his performances soon attracted the attention of Bootle Boys at the age of nine.

By this time he had converted into a centre forward and in one season he even managed to fire an impressive tally of 38 goals!

His passion for the game and ability on the ball meant his coach at the time, Ian Chapman, had no doubts Carra had the qualities to make it in the game.

He said: "I used to call him Billy Whizz because he played with an infectious enthusiasm, wanting to take all the corners, throw-ins, free-kicks and do everything. He was the best player Bootle Boys have ever produced."

While many fans believe his first goal at Anfield came on his first start for Liverpool against Aston Villa in 1997, they may be surprised to see that it actually came years earlier during a regional youth cup final.

"I scored for Bootle Boys when I was about 10 or 11 at Anfield and it was at the Kop End as well," says Carra fondly.

"I cut in on my right foot and hit a shot that went right in the top corner, but the keepers were quite small then

so it wasn't too difficult.

"I think we lost to Liverpool Boys 3-1. They always had the edge on us because they had about 300 other schools to pick from. We only had about 10 or 12 schools in Bootle so we did quite well considering."

It was during his time with Bootle Boys that local scout Harry Hodges spotted him and recommended him to Liverpool.

"He picked up a few of us from Bootle Boys," he recalls.

"I was about 12 at the time. He was the scout for the Liverpool area so he'd been watching Bootle Boys because the best players from all the schools in the area played for them.

"Four or five of us got invited to Liverpool and it went from there really."

Carragher's arrival at Liverpool did not prevent him from continuing to play for his local teams and during his time at Savio High School he had a trial with Sefton Under-14s.

But it was only a brief spell as his ability meant he was destined for greater things and the prospect of a career in football began to take shape when he was selected to go to the National School at Lilleshall.

Teachers who taught Carra show their pride in their ex-pupil

The man who discovered Carra

In August 2006 the man who played a significant part in Jamie Carragher's road to stardom, passed away.

Harry Hodges, who died at the age of 80, was the local scout who spotted Jamie when he was a St James' Primary School pupil playing for Bootle Boys back in the late 1980s.

While Carra has since gone on to achieve success as one of Liverpool's brightest homegrown stars, he has never forgotten just what Hodges did for him.

"He passed away a while ago and I went round to the house with some flowers for the family and it was a sad day," recalls Carra.

"You know, I owe him a great deal and I still know his sons and his grandsons very well.

"It wasn't just me he spotted, I think he picked up Stephen Wright as well.

"He did a lot for Liverpool and obviously he was delighted with how I've done and I kept in touch with him for a long time.

"I was very disappointed to see him pass away but he always did a good job for the club and I'll remember him fondly."

The first taste of Anfield silverware

HAVING seen Roy Evans' first-team suffer FA Cup Final heartache against arch-rivals Manchester United six days earlier the Reds' youth team were hoping to banish the clouds of depression hovering over Anfield when they hosted West Ham in the second leg of the FA Youth Cup Final.

The Reds led 2-0 on aggregate following an impressive win at Upton Park two weeks earlier and an expectant crowd of 20,600 packed into Anfield hoping to see the youngsters claim glory in the competition for the first time in the club's history.

The Hammers were led by current England internationals Rio Ferdinand and Frank Lampard and it was the latter who made an immediate impact when he fired home within the first minute.

But with Carra featuring in a central defensive role in which he would eventually star for the first-team, and Michael Owen showing incredible prowess in front of goal, the Reds dug deep and stormed back to win the match 2-1 and clinch the trophy with a 4-1 victory on aggregate.

Michael Owen closes in on goal while Carra played centre-back in the second leg of the 1996 Youth Cup final

TEAMS
West Ham: Neil Finn, Jason Moore, Joe Keith, Chris Coyne, Rio Ferdinand, David Partridge, Emmanuel Omoyinmi, Frank Lampard, Anthony McFarland, Lee Boylan, Lee Hodges

Liverpool: Roy Naylor, Lee Prior, Phil Brazier, JAMIE CARRAGHER, Gareth Roberts, Mark Quinn, Jamie Cassidy, Stuart Quinn, Andy Parkinson, Jon Newby (Davy Larmour 73)

FA YOUTH CUP FINAL 1996, 1st Leg, May 1, 1996
West Ham 0 Liverpool 2 (Newby 23, Larmour 84)

POST-MATCH reaction
HUGH MACAULEY: "We've proved in this competition already that we're resilient and we can battle and that's what we did against West Ham.

"The senior staff were in the changing room with us and it was smashing to have the manager sitting on the bench in the second half encouraging the lads.

"But that's the way we work at this club, we are always supporting each other when we can."

Stuart Quinn is mobbed by his team-mates after grabbing a goal in the second leg of the 1996 Youth Cup final

TEAMS

LIVERPOOL: Roy Naylor, Lee Prior, Phil Brazier, JAMIE CARRAGHER, Gareth Roberts, Stuart Quinn, Davie Thompson, Mark Quinn, Jamie Cassidy (Eddie Turkington 89), Jon Newby (Andy Parknson 79), Michael Owen

WEST HAM: Neil Finn, Chris Coyne, Rio Ferdinand, David Partridge (Bowen 58), Jason Moore, Emmanuel Omoyinmi, Frank Lampard, Anthony McFarlane, Joe Keith, Lee Boylan (Sains 89), Lee Hodges, Emmanuel Omoyinmi

POST-MATCH reaction

Showing typical bravery and determination Carra shook off a hamstring injury to take his place in the side – although he did not feature in his more accustomed role in central midfield but as a centre-back.

However, post-match comments suggested

FA YOUTH CUP FINAL 1996, 2nd Leg, May 17, 1996 Liverpool 2 (Owen 40, S Quinn 55) West Ham 1 (Lampard 1). Liverpool won 4-1 on aggregate

that the backroom staff of the youth team knew Carra would one day evolve into one of England's top central defenders.

STEVE HEIGHWAY: "Jamie was fantastic. He was so elegant. With Roy Evans using a three centre-back system this could be his position.

"But I'm pleased for all the boys because we are very close to them.

"We showed every facet of football last night. We were down, we battled, and ended up looking terrific."

HUGH MACAULEY: "Jamie's proved his worth in this position and there's a fair possibility that it will be his best.

"He's a natural footballer who understands the game. He's a good passer and he also competes in the air.

"The lads did the club and themselves proud. We are all delighted."

Chairman DAVID MOORES: "It's a tremendous win that puts a smile back on the face of the club."

Looking back . . .

WHEN the class of 2006 reached the FA Youth Cup final last April it marked 10 years since the Reds first won the trophy.

Speaking on the eve of their second FA Youth Cup title Carra looked back fondly on the 1996 triumph and his team-mates at the time.

"There was Roy Naylor in goal; Lee Prior was at right-back, left-back Gareth Roberts who went to Tranmere. Big Eddie Turk at the back with Phil Brazier. Me and 'Little Tommo'

(David Thompson) were in central midfield. Stuart Quinn was on the right and Michael (Owen) played up front with Parky (Andy Parkinson) and Jon Newby, who moved to Bury, and a good friend of mine Jamie Cassidy played on the left hand side. It was a good side; we were very tough to beat. I think we bullied our way to that!

"Michael never played in the first leg of the final where we won away at West Ham 2-0, but he came back for the return. West

The victorious 1996 Youth Cup winning team which included Carra, of course, (back row, second from left), Michael Owen and David Thompson, while the class of 2006 (below) emulated their feat

Ham were a good side. They had Frank Lampard playing and Rio Ferdinand.

"The whole thing about the Youth Cup is it's a big thing playing at the ground and I think it was a big turn-out for us. I think it was just after the 1996 FA Cup final so everybody was a bit down about what happened there, but I think we got about 20,000 to 25,000 there, so it was superb from the supporters. I still see some of the lads out and about in town now, so it's a nice thing to be remembered by."

Dream start to Anfield life starts 10 year love affair

Former Blue celebrates like a true Liverpudlian in front of Kop

FOLLOWING on from his cup winning exploits with the Youth team Carra ended 1996 on a high, signing his first professional contract with the Reds on September 10 and featuring on the substitutes' bench for Premier League matches against Middlesbrough, Arsenal, Sunderland and Leicester City.

The New Year began in earnest and with Roy Evans' men having to contend with a host of injuries and suspensions an 18-year-old Carra was handed his first team debut when he appeared as a 75th minute substitute for Rob Jones in a League Cup Round Five defeat at Middlesbrough.

Three days later he made his first appearance as a first team player at Anfield, when he was given 45 minutes of a goalless draw with West Ham as a second-half replacement for Neil Ruddock.

Finally, with both Michael Thomas and John Barnes missing through injury and suspension respectively, the Bootle-born youngster was rewarded with his first start for the Reds on

January 18, in a clash with Brian Little's Aston Villa.

A solid first half display transformed into a fairytale debut as a teenage Carra broke the deadlock four minutes after the restart when he rose to guide Stig Inge Bjornebye's cross past Mark Bosnich.

The former Everton fan enjoyed delirious celebrations in front of a jubilant Kop – thus beginning a love affair that would stretch over the next decade and beyond.

LIVERPOOL 3 ASTON VILLA 0
January 18, 1997
LIVERPOOL: James, Kvarme, McAteer, Wright.M, McManaman, Collymore, Fowler, Redknapp, Bjornebye, Matteo, Carragher.
Subs: Harkness, Warner, Kennedy, Lee Jones, Thompson.
ASTON VILLA: Bosnich, Southgate, Townsend, Milosevic, Yorke, Johnson, Wright.A, Ehiogu, Tiler, Scimeca, Curcic.
Subs: Joachim, Oakes, Hendrie, Farrelly, Murray.
Referee: Roger Dilkes, Mossley.

ECHO MATCH REPORT EXTRACT, by David Walmsley

"On 49 minutes a dangerous cross from McAteer was headed behind by Ugo Ehiogu at the far post. Bjornebye swung in a corner kick which was met by Bootle-born Carragher with a header that flew beyond Bosnich and into the corner of the goal.

"The Everton fan celebrated ecstatically in front of the Kop..."

CARRA'S REACTION TO HIS FIRST START

DESPITE his goalscoring exploits Carra revealed that he expected to be dropped from the side once first-choice midfielders Michael Thomas and John Barnes were available for selection again.

"I expect to be out of the team next weekend. John Barnes is a world class player who will come back.

"I'm just a kid who has played a couple of games. It will be hard to take but I was always going to be out when the others came back.

"I'll just have to keep my head down and keep working."

CARRA'S REACTION TO HIS GOAL

"WE'D been working on corners on Friday morning.

"Luckily Stig put the ball right on my head and I couldn't really miss. I didn't know what to do afterwards. I just ran away delighted towards the Kop."

THE BOSS' REACTION TO CARRA'S FIRST START

ROY EVANS: "For young Carragher it was a dream come true. Now he must realise that this must happen for the next 10 years."

While Evans was right about Carra featuring for the Reds for the next 10 years, any hopes of him maintaining his fine goalscoring form were optimistic to say the least!

The Houllier reign

The ups and downs of the road to the top under the guidance of Reds' French boss

GERARD Houllier's reign as Reds boss was a series of peaks and troughs - a rollercoaster ride of transition, cup success and Premiership frustration.

From the seventh place finish in his first year in charge through to the sensational cup treble and the difficulty of living up to the demand for progress that it created.

In many ways Jamie Carragher's career made great strides under Houllier and yet it was not until Rafael Benitez entrusted him with a regular place at centre-back that he began to prove his worth as one of the best defenders in Europe.

For while the Frenchman said: "I'll always find room for Jamie in my team," following the arrival of Steve Finnan in the summer of 2003, it was Houllier's tendency to rely upon Carra's versatility that prevented him from truly establishing himself as one of the Premiership's top defenders.

The partnership of Sami Hyypia and Stephane Henchoz was another reason behind his continual deployment in the full-back areas, with the duo forming an outstanding partnership that ensured the Reds no longer suffered from the soft centre that had previously scuppered their trophy hopes.

But while Carra rarely played in his preferred position at centre-back during Houllier's era, he gives his former boss great credit for helping him become the player he is today.

"I was at the club when the manager first came and there are not many of us left now," he said in 2002.

"He saw me play in the first pre-season game and I think he took a bit of a liking to me. ►

It was a rearguard action for most of the game when Liverpool faced Arsenal in the 2001 FA Cup final, but Carra put in a solid shift as this tackle against Sylvain Wiltord demonstrated

'Carragher has been brilliant for us. There will **always** be a place for him in my side'

▶ "He seemed to want to look after my interests off the pitch as well as on it and I remember one day when we were training at Melwood and then heading to Anfield for a game.

"The rest of the players went on a coach but I had to go with the manager in his car and he gave me some advice on how to reach the top and make sure I didn't let it slip away.

"What do I remember? Don't drink between games. I wasn't a big drinker but through an arm round your shoulder, you have to learn that it is not the right way."

That conversation with 'Le Boss' was a pivotal moment for Carra, who took on board what his manager had said and began to work harder on his game – both on the field and off the field. Houllier had recognised his potential and spells at centre-back and right-back followed before an impressive season at left-back saw him enjoy trophy success for the first time, in what was the remarkable treble season.

The final years under Houllier may not have matched the promise of the 2000/01 season but throughout the Frenchman's time at Anfield he continued to place great faith in Carra's defensive qualities and was always keen to respect the club's tradition and ensure the side maintained a scouse heartbeat.

"I have a very solid foundation of local talent at Liverpool and as far as I'm concerned they are staying here for

a very, very long time," he said in 2003.

"They are very committed to Liverpool, even more than some people would know. I know they are committed to the club and the shirt. I put Michael Owen, Steven Gerrard, Danny Murphy and Jamie Carragher all into the same category."

While Owen and Gerrard took the plaudits, the arrival of the likes of Christian Ziege, Markus Babbel, John Arne Riise and Steve Finnan all raised question marks over Carragher's position in the side.

But despite intense competition, his eagerness to improve and fight for his place saw him remain in the starting XI.

However, playing at full-back meant that although he was defensively solid, he needed to provide attacking impetus down the flanks - something he admits

John Arne Riise has an 'unbelievable engine' for getting up and down the wing according to Carra

Carra in the familiar position of leaping into the air with joy at the end of a dramatic European final - on this occasion at the end of the UEFA Cup final against Alaves

Those rare naughty moments...

IN over 400 appearances for the Reds Jamie Carragher's discipline has rarely been called into question.

For while he operates in an age where yellow and red cards are frequently flashed by over-zealous referees, Carra has only received his marching orders on two occasions.

The first came on February 13, 1999, (pictured below) when referee Mike Reed adjudged him to have struck Charlton striker Martin Pringle with his arm in a 1-0 defeat at the Valley.

At the time boss Gerard Houllier launched a passionate defence of his player for what he felt was a harsh red card.

He said: "The decision was wrong and I'd like to know why he made it without giving a yellow card first. I watched the video and it showed nothing happened. I wanted to ask the referee, but he didn't want to see anybody."

In an otherwise unblemished career Carra also received his marching orders in a stormy FA Cup tie at Arsenal in January, 2002.

Mike Riley was the referee this time as Carra, Martin Keown and Dennis Bergkamp were sent for an early bath.

he struggled with to begin with.

"The manager told me that my strength was my defensive play and he told me not to lose that," he said in response to criticism of his forward play in 2003.

"He said that if I could get forward more, then all the better. It is something I have been trying to implement more into my game.

"My crossing is something I'm working on, but I'm never going to be someone who is up and down the flank all the time. You look at John Arne Riise. His engine is unbelievable."

Phil Thompson, who was assistant manager under Houllier, has been delighted by Carra's progress in recent years and admitted that although he is now an outstanding centre-back, his versatility had made him invaluable to the side back then.

"He didn't win too many headlines in those positions but he was always one of the first on the team sheet, he was that important to the side," said Thompson.

It was Carragher's modesty and desire to progress that impressed both Houllier and Thompson – a fact proved by his reaction to the news that the signing of

Markus Babbel would mean he would be moved to left-back.

"He had no qualms at all about it," recalls Thompson.

"In fact, it only served to highlight his professionalism. He would be practicing with his left foot in training every day, both control and delivery. He has always been keen to learn."

Having worked with him for over five years, through good times and bad, few are better equipped than Houllier to assess Carragher's character and his qualities as a defender.

In the run up to the climax of the treble season Houllier summed up why Carra was so integral to his future plans.

He said: "Carragher has been brilliant for us.

"His attitude in training is wonderful and there will always be a place for him in my side.

"I think he looks after himself a lot more now and he always has very good concentration.

"The stability at the back has been great since he has been there. He is a Scouser with a real heart and with players like him you can win things."

When
CARRA
met
RAFA

THE arrival of Rafa Benitez at Anfield heralded not just a new dawn for the club, but for Jamie Carragher as well.

It proved to be the catalyst for a move to his favoured centre-back role and gave him the chance to showcase his defensive talents at the heart of the Reds' defence alongside Sami Hyypia.

It was an important change for Carra because during the six-year tenure of former boss Gerard Houllier he had been largely utilised as a full-back on both flanks with his versatility and commitment to the cause the key factors in his regular inclusion in the Frenchman's starting XI.

But after just one season under the Spaniard, he matured into one of the most respected centre-halves in Europe and was a key figure as the Reds won the European Cup for the fifth time.

Such a transformation does not occur lightly and it is probably the reason why our favourite number 23 regards his current boss as the most important influence on his career.

"The manager has certainly brought me on a lot and maybe the coming years between 27-28 and 31-32 are hopefully the prime for a player," he remarked in October 2004 – just four months into Benitez's reign.

Since then he has been inspirational at the back, establishing himself as the club's number one centre-back and deservedly winning the Supporters' Player of the Year award for 2005.

His was the form of a man who had finally been given the opportunity to perform in his preferred position for a sustained period of time.

"My most comfortable position is centre-back," he said. "That was where I first started for Liverpool but I played left-back when we won a ▶

► few trophies under Gerard Houllier. I have moved around a bit but my favourite position is centre-back."

While Benitez's Liverpool struggled to find any kind of consistency in the Premiership in 2004/05 they were a different proposition in Europe, with the Spaniard's knowledge of the European game proving vital in an inspired run to the final of the Champions League.

Against all the odds the Reds won an epic contest with AC Milan and in the aftermath Carra hailed the influence of his manager.

"What Rafa has done this season surpasses, without any doubt, what any other manager has done," he said.

"Jose Mourinho has won the league for Chelsea in his first season and made a real impact in England. But it doesn't come even close to winning the European Cup in your first season. Now Rafa can go and tell any press conference he likes, as Jose did, that he's the true champion. Mourinho can't say that any more. So is Rafa the special one too? Well, he is to Liverpool fans."

Carra's appreciation of his manager was there for all to see and while he himself deserves credit for his desire to continually improve as a player, he singles out Benitez for making a huge impact on both the club and himself.

> **'It's more difficult for a player to stay at the same club for a long time now and even more so to play the number of games he has. He's played a lot of games and been able to do so at a very high level.'**

In the summer of 2006 he said: "I have had a great deal of help from Rafael Benitez. He has certainly helped us as a back four and he is a big student of the game. He studied the Milan team of the late 80s and early 90s and showed us videos of them and he is determined for us to be as solid and tight as possible."

But what of Benitez's impression of Carra?

Does he hold Carra in the same high esteem?

"Carra is a fantastic person both on and off the pitch," said Benitez, when asked about his relationship with Carragher.

"On the field he is a great player and off it he is a great man to have around the dressing room.

"It's always difficult for the defenders to get praise because usually that's kept for the scoring midfielders or the strikers. He might

Carra is Rafa Benitez's rock at the back, as he demonstrates against Portsmouth (top), while he made his 300th league appearance against Reading

not get the credit he deserves outside of this club but we know how important he is to our team.

"I have worked with some great defenders at Valencia such as Marchena, Pellegrino and Ayala. If you say to me that Ayala was the best then I would say Carragher is not a worse player than Ayala.

"I am sure he will go on to play many, many more games for Liverpool because he is an important part of our future."

That's true and with Carra racking up the appearances, Benitez paid tribute to his defensive stalwart ahead of Carra's 400th game for the club in February 2006.

"It's more difficult for a player to stay at the same club for a long time now and even more so to play the

number of games he has," said Benitez.

"All the time I've known Carragher he's managed to do something even more difficult. Not only has he played a lot of games, he's been able to do so at a very high level and be so consistent.

"For me, it's a fantastic achievement and it's fantastic for me to have someone who is such a good professional."

Carra's 300th league appearance for Liverpool against Reading in November 2006 was another opportunity for the Reds boss to praise Carra.

He said: "Jamie has a fantastic commitment every day in training and in every game he plays. For a manager to see that is brilliant.

"He is a strong character, he's a winner and he loves football. Physically he is always in the best condition, he trains well and is always fit.

"When you sign a player you want one who can play 40 to 50 games each season. Carra is that type of player.

"It is very important for a local boy like Jamie to play a lot of games for his club, I know the fans will be happy. Especially because he is a player who always gives 100%.

"Sometimes even the very best players are not always able to do that, but Carra always plays at his best level.

"Maybe he will make a mistake but it never worries him because he just continues in the same way. Every manager would want him in their team.

"We hope to produce more players with the character of Jamie Carragher."

Liverpool fans wouldn't argue with that.

'Jamie has a fantastic commitment every day in training and in every game he plays. For a manager to see that is brilliant. He is a strong character, he's a winner and he loves football.'

What they said

"Carragher is ten times a better defender than I could ever be. He is a completely different player. He is a great defender whereas I was not. My strengths were on the ball, positional sense and recovery pace. The way he held Chelsea at bay was unbelievable. I'm sitting there in awe of how many times he intercepted, blocked and covered. I think if we look at Liverpool greats over the years - and there have been alot of them - Carragher is up there with the best of them."

- ALAN HANSEN in May 2005

"Since Rafa arrived he has established himself as one of the best centre halves around. Before I came here he was playing left-back. I knew he didn't have a left foot but his left foot isn't bad. He has no problem playing in any position.

"His goalscoring ability is quite poor. His job is to keep clean sheets. I'm sure he would like to get on the scoresheet more but it just doesn't happen."

- JOHN ARNE RIISE in November 2006

"He has been excellent from day one this season and, as a former defender, it is great to see someone play with so much commitment and confidence in his ability. Jamie is not a flashy player, but instead plays to his strengths of tight marking, simple passing and good anticipation, as well as a fair turn of speed."

- MARK LAWRENSON is impressed by CARRA's form at centre-back (Daily Post, October 2004)

"Although you've got a mix of German, Swiss and Finnish in the back four, we all speak to each other in English. The only problem though is that none of us can understand Jamie Carragher!"

- Former Reds defender STEPHANE HENCHOZ

about Carra...

"Jamie Carragher is my player of the season. He has been absolutely superb and wherever he plays he is always consistently good. For Houllier to make him first choice left-back, even though he is not naturally left-footed, when there is a lot of competition there says it all. Competitive and a born winner, he deserves to be first choice for England."

- IAN RUSH acknowledges the qualities of CARRA following his displays in the 2001-2002 season.

"If you wanted to put a player in a Liverpool shirt to go and run through a brick wall for you, then I don't think the fans would pick anyone else but Jamie Carragher and I know the players certainly wouldn't."

- MICHAEL OWEN in 2002

"Steven Gerrard and Jamie Carragher were fantastic. They are the leaders of the team on the pitch and both played brilliantly.
"Steven was influential in the midfield and Jamie was an inspiration at the back - he's had an incredible season and deserves his reward."

- Former Red SAMMY LEE heaps praise on CARRA and Steven Gerrard ahead of the Champions League final.

"Every club needs someone like Carra. You can't buy team spirit and with him around the atmosphere in the dressing room is always brilliant."

- Former Reds keeper CHRIS KIRKLAND.

...and then they

"For me he is Mr Consistent. Throughout the ninety minutes he is always shouting and encouraging the players. He's a leader. In training he is one of the toughest opponents I have ever faced because he is always harassing the opposition and putting in tackles.

"Off the field he is a nice guy too. He's usually quite calm which is a bit different to how he is on the field. He makes people laugh and is always laughing himself. He is a friend of mine. I spend a lot of my time with him and Stevie G.

"You can see how much it means for him to win. He is genuinely interested in the game, I've never seen a player so interested in football. He watches it all the time and is always reading about it. He knows so much about it. I think he lives for Sky Sports News.
- JOHN ARNE RIISE

"Jamie has matured into a world class central defender and deserves every accolade thrown his way.

"He may have enjoyed some fantastic successes on the pitch but he has never forgotten where he has come from. And it is so refreshing that people like him still exist."
- JOHN ALDRIDGE on his fellow Scouser.

"We have big names in our defence which is probably the best in Europe. Liverpool don't have that but they have players to be respected, especially Carragher who is now the third-best defender in the Premiership and has proved very impressive."

- PAOLO MALDINI in May 2005 pre-Istanbul epic.

"What a performance, this guy put in an immense performance, unbelievable."

- STEVEN GERRARD is astounded by CARRA's semi-final performance against Chelsea.

said some more

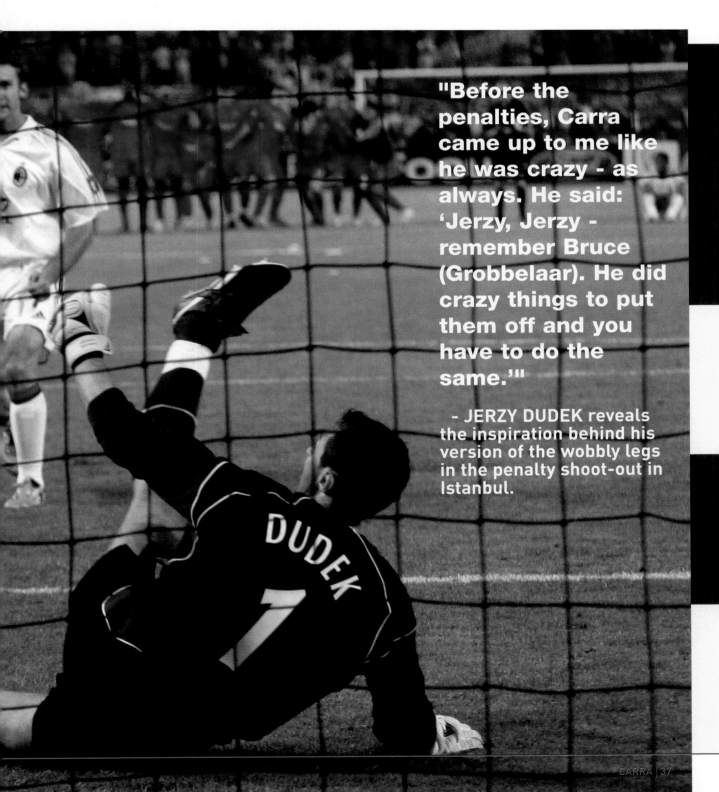

"Before the penalties, Carra came up to me like he was crazy - as always. He said: 'Jerzy, Jerzy - remember Bruce (Grobbelaar). He did crazy things to put them off and you have to do the same.'"

- JERZY DUDEK reveals the inspiration behind his version of the wobbly legs in the penalty shoot-out in Istanbul.

450 not out

Clockwise from top: Carra makes a brilliant block on the line from Alan Smith in 2000,

LANDMARKS seem to come along as frequently as one of his well-timed challenges for Jamie Carragher these days.

Not only is the homegrown stalwart celebrating 10 years since making his Liverpool bow, but in early 2007 he was also due to become only the 19th player in Liverpool's history to rack up 450 appearances for the club – as long as he steers clear of injury.

For Carra it is a great honour to have clocked up such an impressive tally of matches for the Reds, but despite the deserved accolades he is already looking towards the future.

"It's a nice round figure but I think for me 500 is the big one and hopefully I can do that in 12 months time," he said.

"I like to think I will play 50 games a season so it's definitely something I'd like to go on and achieve."

Not content to lead the way in Liverpool's all-time Premiership

tries a shot against Maccabi Haifa, lofts the ball away from Andy Cole in 1999 and performs captain's duties in the 2006 Community Shield

appearances list, Carra also broke through the 300 league game barrier in November's 2-0 win over Reading at Anfield.

And it doesn't stop there!

The month of February should also see him surpass the legendary Ron Yeats' total of 454.

"Obviously if I go past Ron Yeats it will be a great day for me," he said.

"He was a great player, a great centre-half and the Sixties team was

built around him, Ian St John and Roger Hunt.

"I know him very well because he was always around the club and spent years as the chief scout.

"He's one of the names you always think of when you think of Liverpool centre-halves, so to go past him and play more games for Liverpool would be a nice feather in my cap."

Although a 455th game in a Reds shirt would move Carra into 18th place

in the club's all-time appearances list he admits he is unlikely to beat Ian Callaghan's record tally of 857 matches in all competitions.

"I've seen the number of appearances Ian Callaghan made and I can't believe his total," said Carra.

"They must have included five-a-side matches back in the old days with Shankly. I've worked it out and there's no chance of me catching him – even if I play for another ten years!"

Carra with the Liverpool ECHO Sports Personality of the Year award after his performances in 2004

Local hero

ECHO Sports Personality of the Year award shows he's readers' choice too

JAMIE Carragher has earned a lot of plaudits from the national media in recent years, but it's the opinions of those nearer to home that matter most to him.

And it's a good job because it's in his home town where Carra is most appreciated.

More of a team player, Carra had to take the limelight on his own when he was awarded the Liverpool ECHO Sports Personality of the Year award for 2004 at the newspaper's awards night.

Carra was up against Steven Gerrard, Grand National legend Ginger McCain, Olympic medalist Stephen Parry, boxer Robin Reid and Everton goalkeeper Nigel Martyn for the award, but the readers of the paper considered Carra had performed the best that year.

Carra said: "I'm genuinely surprised and delighted I've won.

"I saw the names of the top six candidates in the ECHO and I have to admit I didn't think I was going to win it.

"Stevie had a great year, Nigel Martyn has been outstanding for Everton and I knew one of the candidates won an

Olympic medal, so to be voted the winner out of so many great sportsmen is a great honour.

"It was an up and down year for me because I was injured when it started but I was happy with my form when I returned and it shows that out of something bad, something good can develop."

Carra went on to thank the biggest influences on his career, saying: "Rafa

Benitez has given me a lot of confidence, particularly playing me at centre-half. It always helps when you know the manager rates you.

"Everyone I've worked with at the club deserves a mention, including Gerard Houllier, who was a big influence on me, but my dad deserves the biggest mention because he's been there right from the start and followed me everywhere."

WIN

a framed colour picture of Jamie Carragher in front of the travelling Kop at the Ataturk Stadium on THAT night (as shown below), signed by the man himself

How to enter

ALL you have to do to enter is answer the following question:

Who were the opponents when Carra scored his only goal in European competition for the Reds?

Send your answer, along with your name and address, to: Carragher competition, Sport Media, PO Box 48, Old Hall Street, Liverpool, L69 3EB.

Jamie Carragher,
May 25, 2005

SUPER CARRA

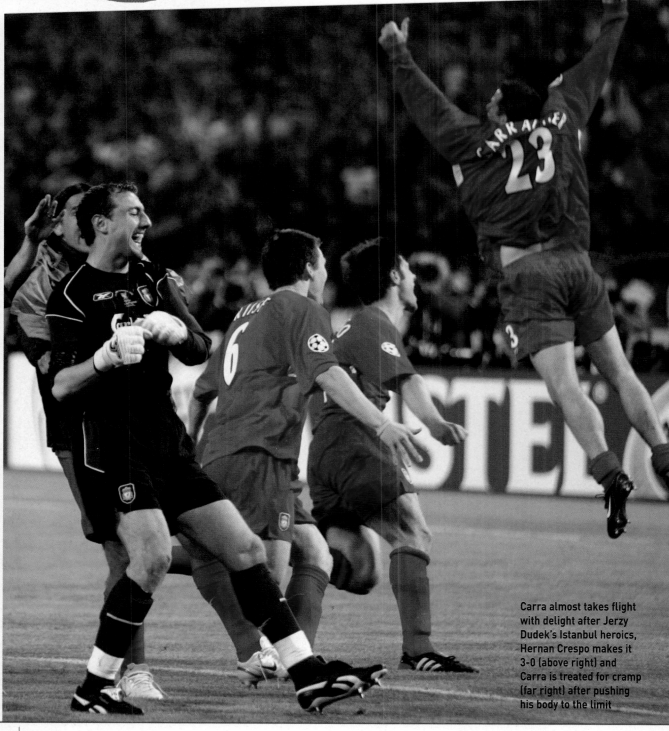

Carra almost takes flight with delight after Jerzy Dudek's Istanbul heroics, Hernan Crespo makes it 3-0 (above right) and Carra is treated for cramp (far right) after pushing his body to the limit

GOES BALLISTIC

THE greatest European Cup final of all time? Probably. The greatest night of Jamie Carragher's career? Most definitely.

For most Reds the legacy of Istanbul will be passed down from generation to generation while the match will take its rightful place in Anfield folklore.

Such was the magic of the night.

But it was not just the events that transpired in the Ataturk that confirmed Carragher's status as the latest in a select group of Anfield legends, but the entire journey to THAT final and a fifth European Cup.

From solid displays in the nail-biting group stages and the comfortable second round triumph over Leverkusen through to an inspired display against Juve in Turin and the titanic 180 minutes against Chelsea – Carra was immense.

The second leg of the semi-final clash with Jose Mourinho's men at Anfield is arguably Carragher's best display in a Reds shirt and led Alan Hansen to say: "It was one of the

The greatest night of Carra's career

great performances from a Liverpool centre-back and over the two legs you could argue that there has never been a better performance from a Liverpool centre-back."

The heroic 1-0 victory on aggregate booked Liverpool's place in Istanbul and was the moment when Carra announced himself as one of Europe's best defenders.

The six minutes of stoppage time were like six years and yet little did we know then that the final itself would prove to be even more dramatic.

Images of a side down and out at half-time but somehow regrouping to take the match into extra-time will live with us forever and not only touched the hearts of overjoyed Reds, but fans across the world.

For many, Jamie Carragher's contribution that night will be defined by the memory of his heroic efforts to hold Milan at bay, while battling against the greater foe of excruciating cramp.

"Unless you've ever had cramp you wont know what I'm talking about but I've broken my leg and I can tell ►

MI-LAN MUST

▶ you the cramp I had in Istanbul that night was worse," said Carra.

"The pain was unbearable. I was screaming and shouting for the physio to get on and sort me out."

Fuelled by the last dregs of adrenalin and a wonder save from Jerzy Dudek the Reds somehow held on for penalties and when Andriy Shevchenko saw his spot-kick saved pandemonium broke out in the Ataturk and in every bar and club in Liverpool.

Just days after the most unlikely of triumphs, back in May 2005, Carra said that he simply felt it was meant to be.

"When Jerzy made that save from Shevchenko I thought we would go on to win it because Shevchenko is a top striker and he put in a top performance," said Carra.

"There was no way he was going to miss that chance. I was just waiting for the ball to hit the back of the net. When it stayed out, you begin to think these things happen for a reason - Stevie Gerrard scoring in the last minute against Olympiakos, coming back from being 3-0 down in a final.

"I tell you what though the best thing the manager did on the night was bringing on The Kaiser (Didi Hamann). What a performance from Didi as when he wasn't there in the first half Kaka caused us all the problems. We couldn't control him when he just kept breaking at our defence but Didi did."

For all the spooky talk of popes dying and royal weddings, something seemed to be driving Liverpool towards their fifth European Cup and for Carra there was one definitive moment that gave him the belief they would win.

"For me, it was probably Eidur Gudjohnsen missing the chance in the final minute when we played Chelsea," he explained.

"For a second, my heart was in my mouth. I thought we had thrown everything away that we had worked so hard for. When his shot whistled past the post, it was the sign that we were going to do it."

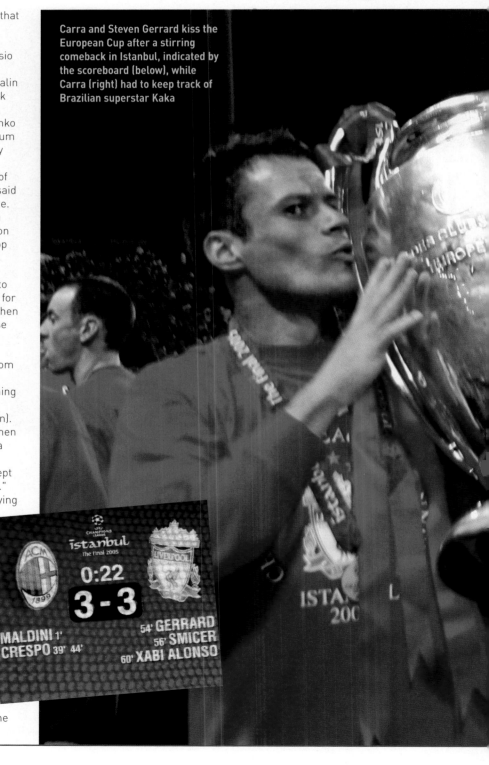

Carra and Steven Gerrard kiss the European Cup after a stirring comeback in Istanbul, indicated by the scoreboard (below), while Carra (right) had to keep track of Brazilian superstar Kaka

istanbul
The final 2005

0:22
3 - 3

MALDINI 1'
CRESPO 39' 44'

54' GERRARD
56' SMICER
60' XABI ALONSO

FEEL ATROCIOUS

What Carra said...

"It is one of the greatest finals of all time and the save Jerzy Dudek made from Shevchenko at the end was unbelievable. I can't believe we've won. He'll be a legend now, not just for the penalties but because of the Shevchenko saves in the game itself. They were unbelievable."

CARRA on Istanbul hero Jerzy Dudek.

"At the end I just took off towards our fans. I couldn't believe it. There were probably 40,000 Liverpool supporters in the stadium and yet the exact place I ran to was where all my family and friends were celebrating. It was unbelievable because I honestly hadn't a clue where they were in the stadium.

"I went so mad that I must have had a bit of a blackout. I just crashed to the floor somewhere and I can't remember a single thing that was going on around me for a few moments.

"I can't stop looking at this Champions League medal - it doesn't even say winners on it! But don't worry, I know what it means."

CARRA recalls the moments following Liverpool's Champions League triumph.

"I'm sure Chelsea did turn up believing they couldn't lose but after hearing the crowd that night I knew we wouldn't lose."

CARRA reflects on one of Anfield's most powerful nights in the Champions League semi-final triumph over Chelsea in 2005.

"All we keep hearing about at this club is the past and what other teams achieved in Europe, so this is our chance to bore everyone for the next 20 years with our own stories.

"We want to create our own bit of history and there's a belief that we can do that. This club's been built on European nights at Anfield and if we do win it, it'll be for a fifth time and we would get to keep the trophy."

CARRA hopes to make some of his own history, pre-Ataturk epic.

"It's a European final and it's all about how many chances you take. Most European finals are only won by the odd goal, there's a lot of 1-0 and hopefully it can be 1-0 to us."

CARRA's pre-match prediction proves to be wide of the mark.

"I'll be on a bender for a week."

CARRA's planned celebration following the win in Istanbul.

Jamie Carragher,
May 25, 2005

He's Scouse, he's sound...

Jamie Carragher is as good as any central defender I've seen wear the red shirt. Emlyn Hughes, Alan Hansen and Ron Yeats were great but Carra can play left and right back too.

Every team needs a Carragher and I reckon him and Daniel Agger will forge a fabulous partnership in the coming years.

He leads by example and would probably be the captain at any other club. He is also desperately unlucky to be at his peak at the same time as John Terry and Rio Ferdinand (hence no regular England spot).

Personally I wouldn't swap Carra for the pair of them!

Dave, Maghull

As the song goes, I think all Reds want a team of Carraghers. He gives 100% effort every week without fail. He would die for the cause.

Sadly he's not seen as a 'fashionable' player, so the England caps are not as regular as they should be.

Nick, Chester.

A true Liverpool legend, born and bred on the Liverpool estates, Carra possesses a fantastic never-say-die attitude and his fighting spirit has earned him recognition across the board in the last few years.

Two memorable moments stick out about Carra for me.

Of course there is the Champions League final where he kept playing on with cramp in both legs.

But the best moment was when he said he wants to spend his whole career wearing the red shirt and would never leave the club.

Everyone red dreams of a team of Carraghers.

Declan, Liverpool.

Jamie Carragher is one of the most reliable defenders ever to wear the Liverpool shirt, representing a work ethic and dedication that is second to none.

The Academy staff can give themselves a pat on the back for their part in producing a defender of the highest quality.

M Saad Qasim, Pakistan.

A true Scouser, he always gives 110% for the club he dearly loves.

He sweats blood for the cause and never gives up.

Jamie is like any typical Scouse fella you would see if you went down the boozer on a match day – down to earth yet with a strong hint of authority.

He is like a player from the Liverpool of old. A grafter, with a strong will and someone the people can relate to.

It's a shame there aren't more like him.

A true red, Kop legend and an inspiration to all Scousers.

Ste, Anfield.

The way Carra has turned himself into one of the best centre-backs in the league is amazing. It's all about hard work and this hard work comes only because of his love of playing for Liverpool FC.

He never looks for sensation. Remember that interview, answering a question with a rhetorical question "is there any bigger club than Liverpool?"

Yes, the memory in Istanbul is one of the best, but also the way he defended during the run to the final is amazing. Watch the game against Chelsea again. You'll hear the name 'Carragher' repeated many times by the commentators.

He's truly a legend.

Perkasa, Jakarta

Carra, to me, is already a Liverpool legend. He was already on his way to becoming a legend by his commitment to the club and fans, but the way he battled through the pain in Istanbul stamped that thought in my mind.

JC is Mr Liverpool and when it comes down to the rough and tumble of the Premiership and the tricky European away ties in remote locations he is always the rock in our defence.

Carra will become a legend for his country if given the chance.

Not many teams can boast having God and JC in the first team squad!

"We all dream of a team of Carraghers!"

David Sumner, Liverpool

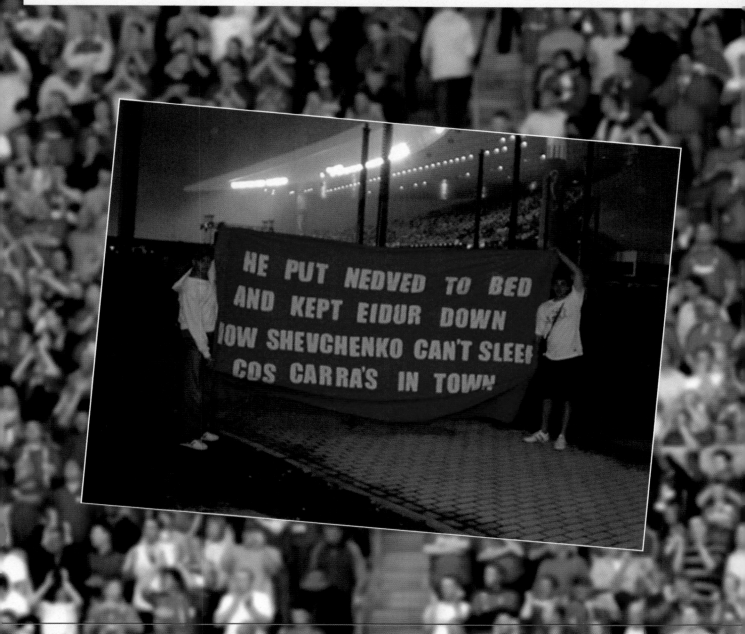

Carra is a legend and that's all there is to it really. He came into the team and bounced around position-wise, but every manager knew there was a job for him, because you can't leave a player like that out.

If I had my ideal representative of what the people of Liverpool were about, or what the club was about, I'd have people watch tapes of him.

The memory of Carra rolling on the floor in extra time after stretching out to block two passes in the Champions League final, when his muscles had already well tightened up, just made you love the guy even more.

Memories of a player doing that just leave you feeling so in awe of the work rate and the skill. There are loads of those memories like that when you think of Jamie Carragher.

Any side in any era would be happy and lucky to have Carra in the first XI. He's absolute class.

Ben, Vancouver.

Jamie Carragher is a modern day Liverpool legend. Apart from Steven Gerrard, no other player has epitomised the spirit of what it means to wear the famous red shirt of Liverpool since the playing days of Graeme Souness.

Carragher is a monster at the back. He marshalls the defence superbly, has no fear of bawling out the goalkeeper or defensive colleagues for any mistakes made and he is probably one of the most versatile players in the game today.

He can play anywhere across the back four and also as a defensive midfielder when called upon.

Carragher has put his own body and health on the line for this club. The Champions League final of 2005 was the measure of the man. His legs had tightened up, he was suffering from excruciating cramp, but he played on and still made some decisive tackles to keep Liverpool in the game.

If there was ever such a thing as a legend before his time, Jamie Carragher is that man.

Simon Pearce, Darlington.

Jamie Carragher is a legend of Liverpool FC because he gives his all in every game he plays in and shows an untouchable passion for his beloved Reds.

He is a true role model for any young player coming through the ranks of any club. The man is a defensive giant, who uses every ounce of energy and willpower to keep the ball out of the Liverpool net.

His passion alone would make him a very good player, but there is no doubt he is talented.

A proud Scouser and Liverpool player, Jamie Carragher is one of the most honourable servants ever to grace Liverpool FC.

Graeme, Northern Ireland.

Carra is a truly great player that always shows 110% effort and commitment to Liverpool FC. It's a shame he's not a regular England player because he's better than Rio Ferdinand, any day of the week.

Gaz, Liverpool.

What can be said about Jamie Carragher that hasn't been said before?

Carra is 100% committed to every game and will sacrifice himself for the sake of Liverpool.

If Steven Gerrard is the heartbeat of Liverpool, Jamie Carragher must be the lungs that breathe passion and pride into the hearts of Liverpool fans around the globe.

He was a Bluenose as a child for his sins, but boy, is he on the correct path now!

Brian Irvine, Northern Ireland.

One of the reasons Liverpool are considered a club of pride and passion, is because they contain one of the most devoted sportsmen ever to have played the game.

Carra never quits, never whines, and never courts the limelight, even though he is the backbone of the team.

One image that has been carved into my memory is of Carra outrunning the pacy Arjen Robben, who had just come on as a sub, against Chelsea in the Champions League semis after playing the whole game. The man is class.

Alan, Croatia.

Carra – season by season

1996-97

Breaking into what many perceived to be the best footballing side in the country at the time was a daunting prospect for an 18-year-old from Bootle.

But after the confidence boost of winning the Youth Cup in the summer of '96 Carragher was determined to make some impression on the first team squad.

1997-98

For Carra the 1997/98 campaign was one of progression.

It was a season in which he firmly established himself as a member of the first team squad, making 23 appearances and enjoying his first taste of a Merseyside derby in a 1-1 draw with Everton at Anfield.

But for the Reds there was further disappointment. They again fell short of

1998-99

The summer of 1998 saw a French revolution at Anfield.

The arrival of highly respected coach Gerard Houllier was an experimental move by the Liverpool board, coming in as joint-manager with Roy Evans, but results suffered and Evans departed.

But any fears that Carra's continued development would stutter under the Frenchman were quickly quelled as

1999-2000

A period of transition was well under way at Anfield as Houllier prepared for the 1999/2000 season by making dramatic changes to the squad.

Among the new signings were Sami Hyypia and Stephane Henchoz - two centre-halves who would signal a shift to a regular right-back position for Carra.

The new-look side struggled at first

2000-01

The 2000/01 season proved to be one that will live long in the memory and was undoubtedly the defining year of Gerard Houllier's tenure as boss.

With the Frenchman again making strong additions to the squad with the likes of Christian Ziege and Markus Babbel, many observers felt it would mean the end of Carra's spell as a first team regular.

2001-02

The Reds started the 2001/02 season high in confidence with impressive victories over Manchester United and Bayern Munich in the Community Shield and European Super Cup respectively.

But trouble struck just a few months into the new campaign when 'le boss' was rushed to hospital during a league match at home to Leeds in October.

Phil Thompson took charge of team

Liverpool had started the season well and were being tipped to be serious contenders to Manchester United's Premiership crown.

A spell on the substitutes' bench gave Carra a taste of what was to come and with injuries and suspensions taking their toll on the squad, the youngster eventually featured in four matches for the Reds

at the start of the new year.

A goal in his first start at home to Aston Villa was the highlight of his year but after his brief spell in the limelight he was forced to wait in the wings for the remainder of the season.

A fourth place finish for Roy Evans' men would mean that the seven-year itch for the

Premiership would continue, but Carra had shown everyone that he was more than ready for the challenge of playing for Liverpool Football Club.

making a genuine challenge for the title and a third place finish again saw them finish outside of the Champions League places.

Carra played every game, except for a suspension after a red card at Charlton.

The Reds missed out on European football with a seventh place finish in the Premiership, but Carra scored his second goal for the club in a 7-1 win over Southampton at Anfield and also made his full debut for England, in a friendly international in Hungary. He was also voted player of the year by Reds supporters.

before pushing on towards the Champions League places.

A late slump meant they missed out on qualifying for Europe's elite competition but Carra made his 100th appearance for the Reds.

It came against Aston Villa in a 0-0 draw at Anfield on March 15 – the same opposition he had made his full debut against three years earlier.

But in typical fashion he rose to the challenge and established himself in an unfamiliar left-back role as Liverpool stormed to a treble cup success and third place in the league.

Carra proved to be a revelation in heroic defensive displays away to Roma, Porto and Barcelona in the UEFA Cup.

Alongside Sami Hyypia, Stephane Henchoz and Markus Babbel he was

part of a defensive unit which was the foundation of the counter-attacking success the Reds enjoyed in their Premiership double over Manchester United and the 4-0 triumph over Arsenal at Anfield.

On top of this, Carra's hopes of winning his first trophy were realised in a penalty shoot-out win over Birmingham in the Worthington Cup in

which Carra confidently slotted in one of the spot-kicks.

It was not long before he was counting medals two and three following an FA Cup final win over Arsenal and an epic 5-4 triumph over Alaves in the UEFA Cup final.

affairs while Houllier underwent massive heart surgery and Liverpool responded with great spirit to reach the summit of the Premiership in December following a 3-1 win over Manchester United.

For Carra it was to be an eventful season.

The arrival of John Arne Riise in the summer had seen him switch back to a

more familiar right-back position after Markus Babbel's season was ended by Guillain-Barre syndrome.

However, despite the joy of making his 200th appearance for the Reds in an FA Cup third round win over Birmingham at Anfield, he was to come under scrutiny in the next round when he was red carded for a coin throwing incident in the holders' 1-0 defeat

against Arsenal at Highbury.

Carra responded well and played in the 2-0 win over Roma which saw the Reds progress into the quarter-finals of the Champions League.

Although they were knocked out in the next round by Bayer Leverkusen, the Reds achieved their best points tally since the inauguration of the Premiership with a second place finish.

Carra – season by season

2002-03

ANOTHER busy summer in the transfer market saw Houllier recruit the trio of Salif Diao, Bruno Cheyrou and El Hadji Diouf for the 2002/03 season.

But while the new signings promised much, they would ultimately struggle to make an impact as a strong start to the season began to fade by the beginning of the new year.

2003-04

HAVING made over 50 appearances in the previous three seasons, 2003/04 proved to be a difficult one for Carra.

The arrival of Steve Finnan meant he was again moved to left-back, but despite the uncertainty over his first team place, worse was to follow.

In only the fifth match of the season he was ruled out of action for four months, when he had his leg broken

2004-05

THE announcement that Liverpool Football Club had secured the services of one of the brightest coaches in Europe breathed fresh optimism through the ranks ahead of the 04/05 season.

Rafael Benitez arrived from Valencia with an impressive CV, having secured two Spanish titles and a UEFA Cup during his reign at the Mestalla.

2005-06

PREMIERSHIP progress was high on the agenda when Liverpool got Rafa Benitez's second season as boss under way.

The Reds comfortably navigated their way past the likes of CSKA Sofia, TNS and Kaunas in the Champions League qualifiers, with Carra scoring his first goal in six and a half years in the 3-1 win in Lithuania.

2006-07

HOPES of a Premiership title charge were high as Liverpool began the new season as many people's favourites to challenge Chelsea.

However, a disappointing run of results on the road saw Rafa's men fall way behind Manchester United and Chelsea at the top of the league with trophy success now looking a more realistic prospect in one of the cup

It was another long season for Carra as he featured in 54 matches, predominantly at right-back.

The Worthington Cup was to be the one consolation in a disappointing season that saw the Reds finish outside the Champions League places, in fifth position.

The 2-0 win over Manchester United at Anfield South was Carra's fifth cup success in five years under Houllier but given the success in previous years the season ended on a low note.

after a challenge by Blackburn's Lucas Neill.

The incident left him fighting to be fit for the final stages of the season.

But in typical fashion he made a quick recovery and returned to action towards the end of January in a Premiership clash at Wolves.

He remained in the side for the rest of the season, switching between both full-back positions when required, and he made his 300th appearance for the club in a goalless draw with Fulham in April.

A season that had began in agony ended well as he secured a place in England's Euro 2004 squad and helped Liverpool clinch fourth spot in the Premiership and a place back in the Champions League.

On a sad note, it was to be Houllier's final season at Anfield and while Carragher enjoyed a number of cup successes under the Frenchman it would be under the incoming Spanish regime that Carra would emerge into an Anfield giant.

But the shock departure of Michael Owen to Real Madrid on the eve of the Premiership's big kick-off was not the start Rafa would have hoped for.

Despite poor performances in the league Liverpool were in fine form in the cup competitions but lost out 3-2 to Jose Mourinho's Chelsea in the Carling Cup final.

By this time Benitez had identified Carra as the perfect partner to play alongside Sami Hyypia at the heart of the back four and he played a key part as the Reds battled past Bayer Leverkusen, Juventus and Chelsea to remarkably reach a Champions League final against AC Milan.

The Reds could only finish fifth in the league, meaning they had to win the Champions League to save their season.

In Istanbul the greatest European final in recent memory took place with Carra playing his part as Liverpool fought back from 3-0 down to win the match in a penalty shoot-out.

To top it off Carra ended the season as Liverpool's player of the season and also finished third in the PFA Players' Player of the Year awards.

Indeed he was in immense form once again as the Reds set a new club record of 11 consecutive clean sheets as they secured 82 points in their league campaign to finish third.

The defence of their European crown came to a halt competitions.

The Reds were imperious in the Champions League group stage however and looked dark horses for a sixth European crown with the knockout stages getting underway in February.

For Carra it looked set to be a season of landmarks.

January marked 10 years since his debut for the club with his 450th appearance in a Reds shirt also likely.

He scored his first goal in the league since 1999 in December's

against Benfica but further cup success was on the cards after Benitez's men beat Manchester United and Chelsea en route to the FA Cup final. That saw a dramatic penalty shoot-out win against West Ham after Carra had scored an early own goal as the match finished 3-3 at full-time.

Carra's season was rounded off as he made England's World Cup squad.

4-0 win over Fulham and could overtake Ian Callaghan's record for the most European appearances for Liverpool, if the Reds make it into the last eight of the European Cup and he avoids injury and suspension.

Brainy Carragher

Carra is the Anfield know-it-all, famed for his Statto-like knowledge of all things football. So on his 10th anniversary as a Reds player, we thought we'd give him 20 questions to put him to the test

Section 1 - All about Carra

1. Who were the opponents when you made your Liverpool European debut?
JC: Celtic in the 1997/98 season.

2. Against which club did you captain Liverpool for the first time?
JC: Yeah I know that. Man City at home. Gerard Houllier, told me the day that I'd be captain because there were a couple of people out injured. I played centre midfield but I didn't play well. Didi Hamann scored two and Michael Owen got the other.

3. Which side have you played against more than any other?
JC: Erm. I think it's probably Chelsea because we've played them in the Champions League and things loads.

4. Which Reds legend said: "Carragher is 10 times a better defender than I could ever be" when talking about your performance against Chelsea in the Champions League semi-final?
JC: Alan Hansen.

5. Which goalkeeper did you score your first Liverpool goal against?
JC: Bosnich.

Section two - All about the Reds

1. Which club did Bill Shankly leave to come to Liverpool?
JC: Huddersfield.

2. Which Liverpool player scored the first goal ever seen on Match of the Day?
JC: It was Roger Hunt wasn't it? Yeah, Roger Hunt.

3. Which team did we lose 1-0 to in our first ever FA Cup final?
JC: Not a clue. Answer: Burnley in 1914.

4. Ian Rush is the club's all-time leading goalscorer, but with how many goals?
JC: (Takes a deep breath) I think it's... is it 346? Who was it who got the league goals record...was it Roger Hunt with 245? Correct as well.

5. Who has scored the most penalties in the Premiership for Liverpool?
JC:(sharp intake of breath) Robbie Fowler?

Section three - International career

1. Who did you make your first England start against and on which ground?
JC: Start? Erm... just trying to think back now – it's either Holland or Sweden isn't it. (pause) Holland. Yeah Holland at White Hart Lane, we got beat 2-0.

2. Who did you replace to come on and take a penalty against Portugal in World Cup 2006?
JC: Lennon

3. How many full England caps do you have?
JC: What when I've started or just when I've played? I've played for England 31 times haven't I?

4. Who do you share the U21s caps record with and how many caps is it?
JC: Gareth Barry and I've got 27 caps.

5. Who did you unofficially captain England against in 2003?
JC: Was it Serbia & Montenegro, yeah.

18/20

Section four - World football

1. Who finished second behind Bayern Munich in last season's (05/06) Bundesliga?
JC: (Pushes another breath out and puts his hand to his head to think) It's either Werder Bremen or Schalke isn't it? (pause) Bremen.

2. Who was the top scorer in Euro 2004?
JC: It was our mate wasn't it? Baros?

3. Which club ended Barcelona's unbeaten start to this season's La Liga campaign?
JC: (Pause) Real Madrid

4. Who were awarded the Serie A title for last season following the match fixing scandal in Italy?
JC: Inter Milan

5. What was the score when Brazil played Japan in their group match in the 2006 World Cup?
JC: 3-1? 2-1? Answer: 4-1 to Brazil. **JC: Just put that I said it was 4-1!**

THEY'RE the Scouse heart of Liverpool Football Club – two local lads from different ends of the same city living every supporters' dream – and close friends both on and off the pitch.

No-one knows vice-captain Jamie Carragher better than skipper Steven Gerrard, who insists our most recent successes under Rafa Benitez owe much to the talents of Carra.

Gerrard has named Carra as his own, personal, player of the year for each of the last two seasons while campaigning for his inclusion in the running for both the PFA and Football Writers' awards.

The two have stood shoulder to shoulder through most of the success Liverpool have enjoyed since the turn of the millennium.

Gerrard is more than happy to pay a glowing personal tribute to someone he rightly regards as a close friend and confidant.

"I said the year we won the Champions League that Carra had had his best season at the club, and it was going to be tough for him, and the rest of us, to better that achievement in 2005/06 but I was proved wrong," Gerrard happily admits.

"He went from strength to strength; he was always consistent, he always led by example and he's one of the main reasons why we've been as successful as we have been in the last couple of years.

"I'm probably biased because he's one of my mates but he's as good as any defender in Europe. He's not one of those players who only turn it on in big games – you get 100 per cent effort, commitment and dedication from Carra every time he pulls on the Liverpool shirt, it doesn't matter who we're playing.

"When I think about how important Jamie's been to us I always think back to Istanbul. He was in agony with cramp but he was still throwing himself into tackles and blocking everything that came his way.

"That's Carra – full of guts.

"I'm always surprised at how little recognition he gets. He deserves to be in teams of the year and certainly should have been in the running for the PFA awards the last couple of years, but the most important thing is that every person at Liverpool – whether it's the players, manager, backroom staff, board or supporters – knows just how important he is to the success here.

"I hope we've got a lot more to celebrate together in the years to come."

JUST CLASS

That's what skipper Stevie thinks about his team-mate Carra

Assistant manager Pako Ayestaran puts his arms around Steven Gerrard and Carra while (left) the two mates enjoy the glory of Istanbul

First l3agu3 start:
January 18, 1997 v
Aston Villa (h),
won 3-0

First l3agu3 goa
January 18, 1997
Aston Villa (h.
won 3-0

Carra -
th3 facts
+ figur35

JAMES Lee Duncan Carragher was born on January 28, 1978, in the Marsh Lane area of Bootle.

His down to earth surroundings would define his character as he made his way from the world of junior football to Liverpool Football Club and the international stage.

Supported by his mother Paula, father Phil and brother Paul, Carra began his football journey as a prolific striker with his local junior side and in the St Joan of Arc Primary school football team.

At the age of 12, the Savio High School pupil was spotted by the late scout Harry Hodges, who recommended him to Liverpool and from here his football education continued as he impressed enough to earn a place at the FA national school of Lilleshall.

A robust tackler with an unquenchable thirst and will to win, Jamie excelled as a central midfielder and in 1996 he was a key member of the Liverpool youth team that won the FA Youth Cup.

His fine performances at youth level saw him sign a professional deal with the Reds in October 1996 and it was not long before he made his first-team debut under Roy Evans in the 1996/97 season.

school att3nd3d:
st. Jam35 RC

3urop3an d3but:
53pt3mb3r 30, 1997
v C3ltic (h), dr3w
0-0

plac3 of birth:
Bootl3

Civic honour:
Award3d fr33dom
of th3 borough
of 53fton in
January 2006

3ngland U215 caps:
27 (joint r3cord
with Gar3th
Barry)

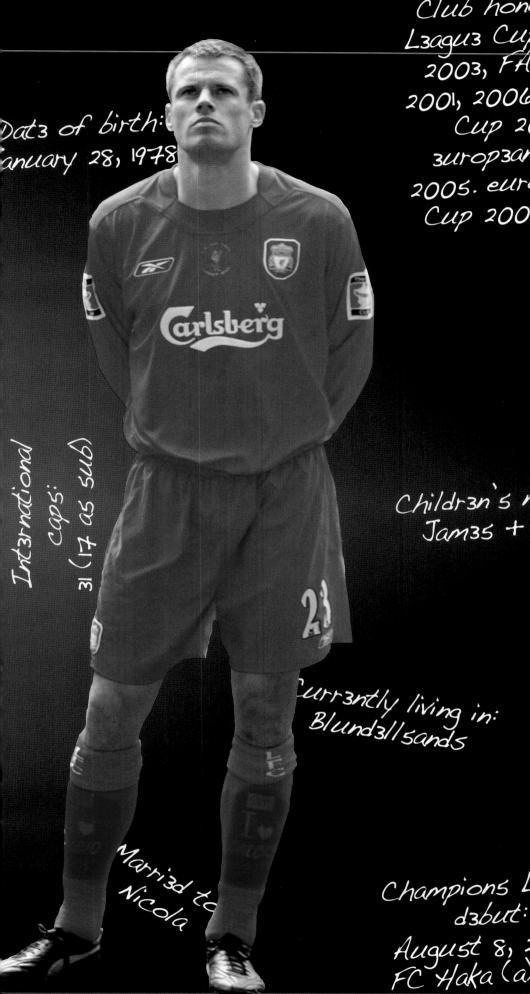

Club honours:
L3agu3 Cup 2001,
2003, FA Cup
2001, 2006, U3FA
Cup 2001,
3urop3an Cup
2005. euro sup3r
Cup 2001, 2005

Dat3 of birth:
anuary 28, 1978

First 3urop3an
goal:
July 26, 2005 v
FBK Kaunas (a),
won 3-1

Int3rnational
caps:
31 (17 as sub)

Childr3n's nam3s:
Jam3s + Mia

Currently living in:
Blund3llsands

Int3rnational d3but:
April 28, 1999 v
Hungary

Marri3d to
Nicola

Champions L3agu3
d3but:
August 8, 2001 v
FC Haka (a), won
5-0

JAMIE Carragher's versatility has been one of the defining features of his career at Liverpool.

Whether you remember his performances as a holding midfielder when he first broke into the first-team, his spell in both full-back positions under Gerard Houllier, or his emergence as one of the best centre backs in Europe under Rafa Benitez, he has probably played in most positions during his 10 years with the club.

But is the famous ditty "We all dream of a team of Carraghers" merely a humorous reflection on his adaptability or has he really managed to play in every position?

With the back four and the central midfield positions accounted for we put the question to him.

"I played right midfield once," he says.

"Tottenham away in 1998. We drew 3-3 and Paul Ince scored an overhead kick.

"The idea was for me to double up with the full-back against Ginola but it didn't really work! I also played at wing back when I first got into the reserves. That was tough because of the running you had to do.

"I haven't played left midfield though. I did when I was a kid but not for Liverpool.

"It was actually one of my first positions when I was a kid before I became a striker."

With all of the outfield positions accounted for, albeit including some games for his junior sides, the prospect of being able to field a team of Carraghers hinges on whether he has ever played in goal.

"No, I've never played in goal," he says.

"Houllier wanted me to go in goal when Westerveld got sent off in the derby in 1999. But Stan Staunton ended up going in and to be honest he did well."

10 out of 11 positions – so close!

But what if he himself could pick the team? Who would feature in Carra's all-time XI?

Goalkeeper: Neville Southall (Everton & Wales) He saved Everton so many times over the years and even now he's still probably the best 'keeper I have ever seen.

Right-back: Cafu (AC Milan & Brazil) It has to be him by virtue that he played in three consecutive World Cup finals.

Centre-back: Franco Baresi (AC Milan & Italy) Baresi bossed simply the best club side I have ever seen - the Milan team of the late 1980s and early '90s.

Centre-back: Marcel Desailly (Chelsea & France) Whenever we used to play against him at Anfield he used to play so well that, to be honest, it was men against boys.

Left-back: Paolo Maldini (AC Milan & Italy) It's easy to take him for granted but he's a legend in his own lifetime.

We all dream of a team of Carraghers, but what team does Carra dream of?

Playing the role of fantasy league manager

What a squad of Carraghers might look like - tough to play against, if a little strange to look at!

Right-midfield: Zinedine Zidane (Real Madrid & France) I would include four in midfield and that would have to include Zidane, the best player of the modern era.

Centre-midfield: Graeme Souness (Liverpool & Scotland) 'Souey' had everything. You don't see many players who can put their foot in and also dictate a game in the way he could. Graeme was like Roy Keane and Glenn Hoddle rolled into one.

Centre-midfield: Roy Keane (Man United & Republic of Ireland) And talking of Roy Keane, I'd have him alongside Souey at the heart of midfield. The Man United skipper may be a little short of Souness in the passing department but he has so much drive.

Left-midfield: John Barnes (Liverpool & England) Barnesy is simply the best player I've played with and trained with. It was a real pleasure and privilege to be there with him. He was phenomenal.

Centre-forward: Marco van Basten (AC Milan & Holland) Probably the best striker I've ever seen. He wasn't just a goalscorer; he could hold the ball up superbly and had great skill.

Centre-forward: Kenny Dalglish (Liverpool & Scotland) Kenny would play just off Van Basten. Liverpool were obviously the most successful team in British football and to me, he was the best player who ever played for Liverpool.

Substitutes: Thierry Henry (Arsenal & France) & Jamie Carragher (Liverpool & England) What a great player Thierry Henry is - I'd say he's the best player ever to play in the Premiership, probably just ahead of Alan Shearer. And, as it's my team, I'd put myself on the bench as well because I can play in a number of positions - not that it would be easy to get in this team!

*Interview originally featured in FourFourTwo magazine

Carra's all-time XI

Southall

Cafu

Baresi

Desailly

Maldini

Souness

Keane

Zidane

Barnes

Dalglish

Van Basten

10 finals in 10 years

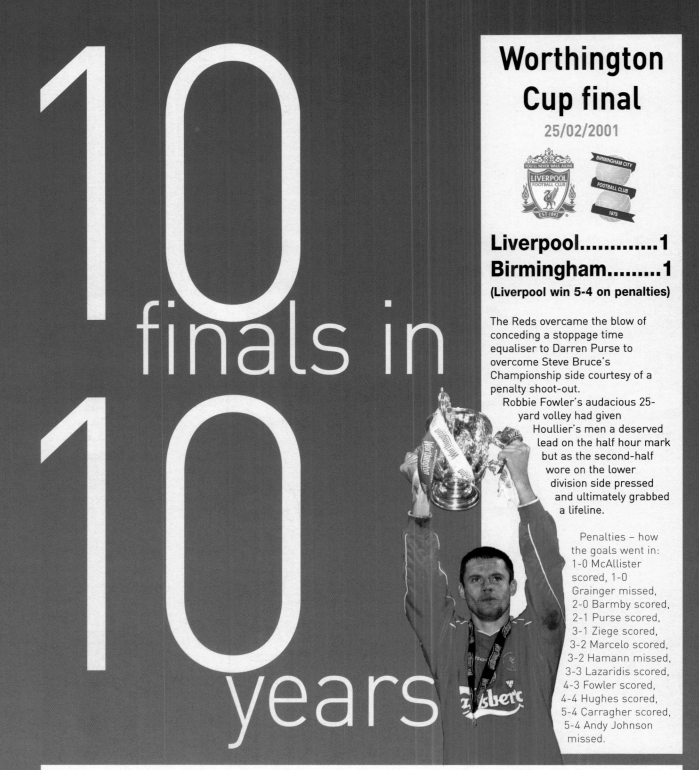

Worthington Cup final

25/02/2001

Liverpool..............1
Birmingham.........1
(Liverpool win 5-4 on penalties)

The Reds overcame the blow of conceding a stoppage time equaliser to Darren Purse to overcome Steve Bruce's Championship side courtesy of a penalty shoot-out.

Robbie Fowler's audacious 25-yard volley had given Houllier's men a deserved lead on the half hour mark but as the second-half wore on the lower division side pressed and ultimately grabbed a lifeline.

Penalties – how the goals went in:
1-0 McAllister scored, 1-0 Grainger missed, 2-0 Barmby scored, 2-1 Purse scored, 3-1 Ziege scored, 3-2 Marcelo scored, 3-2 Hamann missed, 3-3 Lazaridis scored, 4-3 Fowler scored, 4-4 Hughes scored, 5-4 Carragher scored, 5-4 Andy Johnson missed.

MOST professional footballers dream of one day running out at Wembley (or more recently Cardiff) and playing a starring role as the club they love clinch victory in one of the most memorable cup finals of all-time.

To achieve it once would be beyond most players' greatest hopes and to feature in two would be a dream come true.

For players at Liverpool it is par for the course, but even some of the Reds legends from the halcyon days of Shankly, Paisley, Fagan et al would struggle to match Carra's record.

The tough-tackling number 23 has featured in a showpiece final on no fewer than 10 occasions during a decade of tremendous cup success with his hometown club - for the mathematically challenged among you that works out at a cup final for every season.

The living legend has rarely lost on the big stage either, with an enviable record of eight wins and just two defeats during this period.

But at first he must have wondered if it would ever happen.

When he broke into the side the Reds were about to undergo a transition from the free-flowing football of Roy Evans' reign to the French revolution under Gerard Houllier. Cup finals in Cardiff were not the regular trip we have become so accustomed to.

During these dark days Carra and Co's cup hopes were continually undone by bad luck and poor performances leaving fans dreaming

FA Cup final

12/05/2001

Liverpool............2
Arsenal...............1

A one-sided cup final appeared to be going the way of Arsene Wenger's men after Freddie Ljungberg opened the scoring for the Gunners just after the hour mark.

But Michael Owen had other ideas and after pouncing on Markus Babbel's knock-down to level the scores with seven minutes to go, he went on to fire home a sensational winner with just two minutes left, after outpacing the Arsenal defence and unleashing a left-footed strike beyond David Seaman.

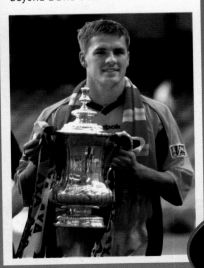

UEFA Cup final

16/05/2001

Liverpool............5
Alaves.................4

(After extra time)

The Reds looked set to comfortably complete their cup treble when they raced into a 3-1 interval lead courtesy of goals from Markus Babbel, Steven Gerrard and Gary McAllister's penalty.

However, a second-half fightback saw Javi Moreno hit a double to bring the Spanish side level. Substitute Robbie Fowler then drilled a superb fourth to give the Reds the lead again.

But in injury time former Manchester United forward Jordi Cruyff capitalised on Sander Westerveld's error to take the game many pundits predicted would be one of the most dull finals in history, into extra-time at 4-4!

The Reds were preparing themselves for their second penalty shoot-out final of the season when Gary McAllister curled a devilish free-kick into the box and Delfi Geli headed into his own net to hand the trophy to Liverpool with a golden goal winner.

Super Cup final

24/08/2001

Liverpool.............3
Bayern Munich....2

Two weeks after defeating Manchester United in the Community Shield in Cardiff, Gerard Houllier's men clinched their fifth trophy of the year when they overcame the European champions.

Goals from John Arne Riise, Emile Heskey and Michael Owen gave Liverpool a commanding second half lead but a late Bayern fightback saw them reduce the arrears to leave the Reds holding on for victory.

Cup final record

Pld	W	L	F	A
10	8	2	24	19

of the feast of honours that they had recognised as a birthright during the 1980s.

But in 2000/01 it all changed in dramatic fashion.

The barren run in his first four seasons with the club came to an incredible end as Liverpool clinched a cup 'treble' for the first time in history.

Carra even scored a penalty in a high-pressure penalty shoot-out in the first leg of the remarkable cup adventure, when the Reds beat

Birmingham City to win the Worthington Cup and secure the club's first trophy in six years.

Inspired by their success and the Indian summer of veteran Gary McAllister, the Reds powered their way towards both the FA Cup and UEFA Cup finals.

An unbelievable late double from Michael Owen snatched victory from the jaws of defeat against Arsenal while one

of the greatest European finals of all-time against Spanish minnows Alaves, ended with the Reds clinching the cup treble at the end of an epic nine-goal thriller.

From there the trips to Cardiff multiplied and with each final the matches grew in intensity and became even more dramatic.

The disappointments have been few and far between and with the spirit of Istanbul now firmly rooted in the side's mentality, few would bet against more success in years to come.

Worthington Cup final

02/03/2003

Liverpool............2
Manchester U.....0

Gerard Houllier's men continued their good form against their arch-rivals with a richly deserved win at Anfield South.

Steven Gerrard's deflected effort put them in the ascendancy and with Jerzy Dudek in inspired form, they sealed the win when Michael Owen broke clear to fire the ball past Fabien Barthez.

Carling Cup final

27/02/2005

Liverpool.............2
Chelsea..............3
(After extra time)

The Reds suffer a rare defeat in Cardiff despite taking a first minute lead courtesy of John Arne Riise's powerful volley.

Steven Gerrard's own goal gifted Chelsea an equaliser late on and the Londoners go on to clinch victory despite Antonio Nunez heading his first and only goal for the club with seven minutes remaining.

European Cup final

25/05/2005

Liverpool.............3
AC Milan.............3
(Liverpool win 3-2 on penalties)

The greatest European Cup final of all-time?

Sheer theatre unraveled before the eyes of the fans who crammed into the packed Ataturk Stadium to witness the comebacks of all comebacks.

Dead and buried at half-time, three goals in six minutes transformed the game and saw the Reds take the Italian aristocrats to a penalty shoot-out.

Stevie G's header, Vladi's last goal for the club, Xabi's rebound, Jerzy's wobbly legs and the heroic display of Carra despite suffering with chronic cramp, are all moments etched in the history of Liverpool Football Club.

Penalties – How the goals went in: 0-0 Serginho missed, 1-0 Hamann scored, 1-0 Pirlo missed, 2-0 Cissé scored, 2-1 Tomasson scored, 2-1 Riise saved, 2-2 Kaka scored, 3-2 Smicer scored, 3-2 Shevchenko missed.

Steven Gerrard lifts the Worthington Cup with Michael Owen in 2003 after their goals sank Manchester United, while Gerrard couldn't hide his anguish after losing to Sao Paulo in the World Club Championship final (below)

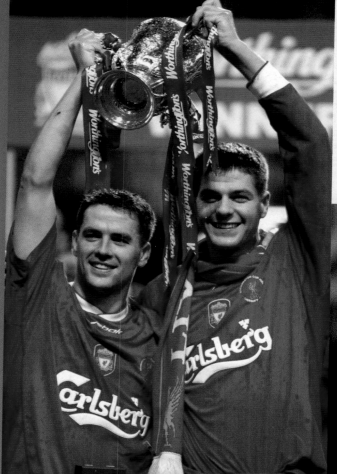

Super Cup final

26/08/2005

Liverpool............3
CSKA Moscow.....1

(After extra time)

A proud moment for Carra after he captained the side to a second Super Cup triumph in four years.

Substitute Djibril Cisse took the match into extra-time when he equalised with eight minutes remaining.

The Frenchman then gave Liverpool the advantage before setting up Luis Garcia to complete a turnaround and give Liverpool the trophy.

World Club Championship final

18/12/2005

Liverpool............0
Sao Paulo............1

The European champions missed out on becoming the World champions for the first time in the club's history despite dominating throughout the match.

Mineiro's goal in the 27th minute proved decisive as the Brazilians held on to secure a surprise victory.

FA Cup final

13/05/2006

Liverpool............3
West Ham..........3

(Liverpool win 3-1 on penalties)

The Steven Gerrard final began on a sour note for Carra after diverting a cross into his own net to give the Hammers the lead.

Dean Ashton then put Alan Pardew's men two up before goals from Cisse and Gerrard drew Liverpool level.

But then a freak goal from Paul Konchesky seemed to have won the cup for West Ham until Steven Gerrard's sensational 30-yard thunderbolt took the game into extra-time.

Cue another penalty shoot-out and another Liverpool cup success.

Penalties – how the goals went in: 1-0 Hamann scored, 1-0 Zamora missed, 1-0 Hyypia missed, 1-1 Sheringham scored, 2-1 Gerrard scored, 2-1 Konchesky missed, 3-1 Riise scored, 3-1 Ferdinand missed.

Carra congratulates Steven Gerrard after his outstanding contribution to the 2006 FA Cup final

Born to lead

The captain behind the captain - the voice that rallies the troops

AMIDST the passion and the spine-tingling sound of the Kop in full song, a familiar voice can be heard rallying the troops on a match day at Anfield.

But it is not the cry of club captain Steven Gerrard about to take his side into battle.

For while the legendary number eight has led by example by inspiring us to the epic triumphs of both Istanbul and last season's FA Cup success, he does not, by his own admission, possess the vocal tenacity of the likes of Emlyn Hughes and Graeme Souness.

Instead the choice words with team-mates and cries of 'Get out, get out!' are the shrill tones of vice-captain Jamie Carragher.

The tough-tackling number 23 embodies all the traits of what traditionalists perceive to be the true attributes required to captain a football club.

Strong and determined with a visible passion to raise the game of those around him, Carra is the perfect deputy when Steven Gerrard is unavailable.

Recognised throughout the club for his leadership qualities it wasn't long before he followed in the footsteps of

some of the Reds' most legendary names when he captained the side for the first-time in a 3-2 win at home to Manchester City on September 9, 2000.

He has since worn the armband on countless occasions and has even joined the elite group of players to have raised a trophy as Reds captain, when he deputised for the injured Gerrard in the European Super Cup win over CSKA Moscow on August 26, 2005.

A year later, on August 13, 2006, he raised the Community Shield alongside Gerrard after he had started the 2-1 win over Chelsea as captain, while the club skipper began the match on the bench.

Carra leads the Reds in Bordeaux in the absence of Steven Gerrard while (right) he captains the side for the first time against Man City in 2000

Biggest lift of Carra's life

EUROPEAN SUPER CUP
Friday, August 26, 2005

Liverpool (European champions).......3
Cisse 82, 103, Garcia 119
CSKA Moscow (Uefa Cup winners)....1
Carvalho 28
(after extra time)

CARRA'S dreams of lifting a trophy for Liverpool were realised after substitute Djibril Cisse turned the match on its head.

CSKA hitman Daniel Carvalho had given the Uefa Cup winners the lead on 28 minutes when he rounded Pepe Reina and slotted the ball in from a tight angle.

The Reds went into the break trailing 1-0 and continued to frustrate their travelling fans in the second period with Luis Garcia missing a series of good opportunities.

With just 11 minutes remaining Benitez brought on Djibril Cisse and within three minutes he had levelled the score.

A long ball from Reina was flicked on by Garcia and when a CSKA defender fired a clearance against the Frenchman's hand, the ball looped over goalkeeper Akineef and allowed Cisse to run through and smash the ball into an empty net.

Having looked set to leave Monaco empty-handed the Reds found a new lease of life in extra-time and within 12 minutes of the restart they had taken the lead.

Dietmar Hamann's long ball again caused problems in the CSKA defence

and after Cisse drilled his first attempt at the keeper the ball fortuitously rebounded to the Frenchman, who gleefully slid it home.

The Russians pressed in the hope of taking the contest to a penalty shoot-out but when Cisse broke down the right in the final minute he crossed the ball for Garcia who nodded the third to secure victory for the Reds.

Liverpool: Reina, Josemi, Riise (Cisse 79), CARRAGHER (capt), Hyypia, Finnan (Pongolle 55), Garcia, Alonso (Sissoko 71), Hamann, Morientes, Zenden.

CSKA Moscow: Akinfeev, Ignashevich, A Berezutsky, Berezutsky, Ordia (Gusev 90), Carvalho, Vagner Love, Krasic (Dudu 85), Zhirkov (Semberas 66), Aldonin, Rahimic.

Skipper's reaction

"It is nice to win this trophy and we're looking to win as many as we can now.

"We were without Stevie tonight, but it was nice to lift the cup and it was a great honour.

"To captain Liverpool in any game is special, but to do it in a final, particularly an occasion like this, is one of the proudest nights of my life.

"Obviously, the most important thing is to win the game. We were looking to put in a good performance because, as the gaffer has said, winning any trophy is what it's all about for us."

Words of

WHEN I say life, I mean it. I want to stay here. When I say that, it's not talk, I really mean it.

I mean I'm not kidding myself, I don't think I'm going to go any higher than Liverpool. If your club's in the Champions League that's the ultimate and obviously you want to win trophies.

"I've been lucky enough to do that here in the past and I want to win bigger trophies now, the Champions League and the Premiership.

"We're not at that level yet but the new manager, if he can bring in a few more players, can get us to that level. I've never even thought about leaving."

Carra reveals his lifetime commitment to Liverpool (March 2005).

"Of course there's expectancy. We've got so many ex-player in the media, no matter what we do, they've always done more so it's difficult to make your own history. But that's the club you play for. You need a certain mentality to be a Liverpool players because you face a lot of criticism. We seem to have a crisis every year – lose a couple of games and it's a crisis."

Carra on how playing for Liverpool can sometimes be a burden.

"There's no point sulking about it. There's not a lot you can do, except impress the manager in training and in games. Or find out his (Finnan's) address and send the boys round!"

Carra responds with typical good humour following the arrival of Steve Finnan.

"We'd all like to be centre-forwards and score goals. We'd all like to play where we want but it's up to the manager to decide."

wisdom

Carra shows what he could be doing regularly if he was a centre-forward, by scoring against Fulham

"Phil Thompson turned around to Michael Owen and said 'I don't fancy Carra with this one'.
"But you know how it goes with pens, sometimes they go in for you and sometimes they don't."

Carra reveals the Reds backroom staffs' lack of faith in his ability from the spot in the 2001 Worthington Cup success over Birmingham City.

"Where would I like to play? In the team!

"Internationals can't even get on the bench and you have to just be happy just as long as you are getting a game for Liverpool.

"People can have their opinions about my best position. We'd all like to be centre-forwards and score goals. We'd all like to play where we want but it's up to the manager to decide.

"Playing at left-back means I'm not on my strongest foot but right-back is exactly the same position. It's just the other side of the pitch."

Carra proves he is the master of stating the obvious when asked about his best position in May 2001.

"As far as I'm concerned, Steven Gerrard is the best player in the world today. I wouldn't swap him for anyone, even Ronaldinho."

Carra gives his skipper the ultimate compliment.

"When the news came through on the TV, I nearly choked on my cornflakes."

Jamie Carragher, overjoyed at the news of Steven Gerrard's transfer u-turn.

'Win first, talk later' is Rafa Benitez's attitude, according to Carra

"The players who set the record in 1987/88 were top players. They were players who had won two or three European Cups and league titles. We've won just one European Cup.

"Statistics are nice, they show we are doing a good job at times, but it's all about silverware."

Carra plays down the clean sheet record achieved in December 2005.

"I don't go on the websites or anything but I believe there's murder there after a game if we have got beaten.

"But I'm not kidding people. If the team were to get beaten then I know I'd

"I don't think any of us will be going to the FA Cup final to showboat or take it easy. If there is even the slightest sign of that, I will be having a word." **– Carra, May 2006**

be one of the first to get criticised!"
Carra in 2003.

"There may be more skilful players in the squad, but no one can ever say I don't give 100%."
Carra on his commitment to the Liverpool cause.

"Of course I'd love to play in my proper position and be given the chance to show what I can do there but there's no point moaning or sulking about it.

"John Terry and Rio Ferdinand were two of our best performers during the tournament and I'm well aware that

one of the main reasons I was in the squad was because of my versatility so I can't start complaining when I'm playing right-back or wherever.

"I believe I'd do a better job at centre-back because that's my position but that's not a criticism of the manager.

"There are only 11 places in the team and he has to pick the team he thinks is right for England. It's not about individuals."
Carra after the 2006 World Cup.

"Our manager always tells us: 'If you think you are better than them, make

sure you beat them first, then say it afterwards.' He won't tolerate anyone saying it beforehand, you can be sure of that.

"It will ruin a lot of summers if we don't win it, and I'm not having that. It's the World Cup after this, and it will be pretty depressing if I have to link up with the other England lads having lost the FA Cup.

"I don't think any of us will be going there to showboat or take it easy. If there is even the slightest sign of that, I will be having a word."
Carra talking pre-FA Cup final epic with West Ham, May 13, 2006.

And the goals...

... they did flow

(like treacle!)

The shoot-outs

February 25, 2001 v Birmingham City (N) Worthington Cup Final 1-1aet – Won 5-4 on pens

AN enthralling contest with Trevor Francis' Birmingham City ended all square after extra-time leaving the Reds to test their luck in a penalty shoot-out.

With the scores level entering sudden death many Reds could be forgiven for closing their eyes when they saw Carra stepping up to take the penalty.

But oh ye of little faith – a mammoth run up was followed by a superb strike that arrowed into the top right-hand corner giving Ian Bennett no chance.

Carra's successful spot-kick proved significant as the next penalty saw Sander Westerveld deny Andy Johnson to win the trophy for Liverpool.

Carra proves a spot king against Birmingham in the 2001 Worthington Cup final

December 4, 2002 v Ipswich Town (H) League Cup Round Four 1-1aet – Won 5-4 on pens

AN under-strength Liverpool were forced to come from behind to earn a 1-1 draw after extra-time against Ipswich Town at Anfield.

On as a second-half substitute Carra stepped up to take the Reds' fourth penalty and continued his prolific run from the spot with a familiar full speed ahead run up and a well struck effort into the right hand side of the goal.

How they went in...

one

January 18, 1997 v Aston Villa (H) Premiership - Won 3-0

CARRA capped his first start for the Reds with a dream goal in front of the Kop. Stig Inge Bjornebye fizzed a dangerous corner in from the right and Carra stooped unmarked to power the header beyond Bosnich.

A first start and a first goal – was this a sign of things to come...?

Carra gets a goal against Aston Villa at Anfield after earning his first start

two

January 16, 1999 v Southampton (H) Premiership - Won 7-1

ERM...no. Two seasons later the defensive midfielder was proving he was a jack of all trades and was now operating at right-back.

With the Reds 4-1 ahead, Paul Ince touched a free-kick into Jamie Redknapp's path and when his stinging drive looped up off Paul Jones' knee Carra was on hand to tap the ball home from three yards out.

three

July 27, 2005 v FBK Kaunas (A) Champions League Qualifier - Won 3-1

LIVERPOOL'S player of the season achieved so much during the 2004/05 season – except the glory of his first goal in six seasons.

But three matches into the defence of the European Cup he had fans rubbing their eyes in disbelief when he met Steven Gerrard's left-wing corner at the near post and diverted the ball underneath the goalkeeper and in off a defender's knee to score his first goal away from Anfield!

four

December 9, 2006 v Fulham (H)
Premiership - Won 4-0

JUST when it seemed like Carra was never going to score in the league again, he popped up with a striker's finish in the home league match with Fulham.

With Sami Hyypia rested, Carra and Daniel Agger were the Reds' main threats at set-pieces and the two combined from a corner to make it 2-0.

Agger met the ball with a glancing header and Carra was waiting at the far post to steer the ball home.

Carra celebrates a goal against Middlesbrough, but Michael Owen took the credit

The one that got away

December 26, 1998 v Middlesbrough (A)
Premiership - Won 3-1

WHEN Paul Ince headed Jamie Redknapp's right-wing corner back into the danger area, Carra pounced to prod the ball goalwards from 10 yards out.

The ball found the corner of the net and young Carra ran away to celebrate with Phil Babb, Robbie Fowler and Steve Staunton.

But at the same time Michael Owen was celebrating by the corner flag and later claimed he got the final touch.

The goal was credited to Owen and the Reds went on to win 3-1 with Vegard Heggem netting a memorable solo goal late on.

Carra punches the air after his goal against Southampton

TO lead the way and be ranked above the likes of Alan Hansen and Ron Yeats in one of Liverpool Football Club's all-time leading lists would usually be seen as a major honour and a magnificent achievement.

But not when you are talking about topping the club's own goals chart!

Unfortunately for Carra this is the case after his own goal in the FA Cup final last May gave him the outright lead with five own goals to his name.

He is also the only Reds player to have ever netted a double own goal after his misfortune against Manchester United in a 3-2 home defeat in 1999.

Having scored at the right end on just three occasions during his 10 years with the club, Carra needs to discover a goalscoring touch soon if he is to end up with more goals in his Liverpool career than own goals.

Nobody's perfect

Carra tops all-time Anfield list ...for scoring own goals

The own goals

TOTTENHAM 2 LIVERPOOL 1,
December 5, 1998
Carra's first own goal for the club was a spectacular one.

Chris Armstrong won a tussle with Phil Babb on the right and drilled a low cross into the box. With Les Ferdinand lurking, Carra attempted to intervene, but as he slid in he powered the ball beyond David James to put Spurs two up.

LIVERPOOL 3 TOTTENHAM 2, May 1, 1999
With the memory of the own goal still fresh in his memory Carra went into the return match with Spurs hoping that lightning would not strike twice.

Unfortunately it did.

Steffen Iversen broke down the right-hand side and played a short ball into the edge of the six yard box.

Chris Armstrong looked set to score at the near post but when he missed his kick, the ball struck Carragher and deflected through Brad Friedel's legs to give Spurs a 13th minute lead.

LIVERPOOL 2 MAN UNITED 3,
September 11, 1999
A nightmare game for Carra.

His first own goal came when Dwight Yorke capitalised upon a poor clearance and fed Ryan Giggs on the left. The Welshman fired in a dangerous cross and as Carra stretched to put it behind at the near post, he diverted it into his own net to give United the lead at the Kop end.

But it got worse for our favourite number 23. A David Beckham free-kick from the right was met by Henning Berg and when his powerful header struck Rigobert Song it rebounded back onto Carra and into the net.

LIVERPOOL 3 WEST HAM 3 (Liverpool win on penalties), FA Cup final, May 13, 2006
The Reds gave the ball away in their own half and allowed Dean Ashton to turn and play a superb ball out wide for Lionel Scaloni.

The Argentinian fired a low ball into the box and as Carra rushed back to try and cut out the danger, he stretched and turned the ball past Pepe Reina at the near post.

All-time own goal list

1) Carra (5)
2=) Ron Yeats (4)
2=) Alan Hansen (4)
3=) Tommy Smith (3)
3=) Dick White (3)
3=) Alec Lindsay (3)
3=) Neil Ruddock (3)

Carra can't believe his bad luck after scoring an own goal in the 2006 FA Cup final as West Ham's Dean Ashton celebrates

Lucas Neill is dismissed after his lunge was punished with a red card, but Carra was left with a broken leg

He had his leg broken, but wanted to play on!

WHILE the majority of his ten years at Anfield have been blessed with a series of magnificent highs, the 2003/04 season proved to be one of the most frustrating periods in Jamie Carragher's career.

Having started the season in the side despite the presence of new arrival Steve Finnan, Carra looked all set to maintain his place and earn a position in England's Euro 2004 squad.

But that all changed on September 13, when the Reds travelled to Ewood Park for a Premiership clash with Graeme Souness' Blackburn Rovers.

A challenge in the 17th minute from Blackburn's Lucas Neill saw the Australian receive a red card and left Carra with a broken leg.

His determination to carry on was typical of the man and was a moment which cemented his place in the hearts of all Reds fans.

Liverpool went on to win the match 3-1 but it was of scant consolation with both Carra and striker Milan Baros picking up long-term injuries.

At the time Carra was more concerned about the fact he would lose his place in the side and even found time to joke about it.

"My mum came round to see me and said I can start a competition with my baby son James," he said. "We're going to see who can start walking first."

Just over three years later and he is quick to laugh off the reputation his

'If I'd known I'd broken my leg I probably would have stayed down and done the sensible thing'

attempts to play on created.

"I know the fans made a big deal of that but I didn't know that I'd broken my leg," he recalled.

"You don't know what you've done!

"It was a bad tackle and it was very painful. The initial impact was bad but then it eases off a little and you think, 'well I'll just try and stand up' and you

try to give yourself a minute or two.

"I tried to put a bit of weight on it but I could just feel that it wasn't 100% right.

"I mean if I'd known I'd broken my leg I probably would have stayed down and done the sensible thing and gone off.

"But I was desperate not to come off. I ended up being carried off and it wasn't until the next day that I found out what I'd done.

"Our doctor had gone up to the hospital with Milan Baros, so I didn't see him until the next day at Melwood.

"He looked at it for two minutes and said 'we need to get you to hospital, I think you've broken your leg.'"

While it was feared Carra would miss up to six months of the season, he returned in double-quick time and was back in the side for the 1-1 draw against Wolves on January 21.

His form between that match and the rest of the season earned him his place in the England squad and underlined a remarkable turn around in fortune.

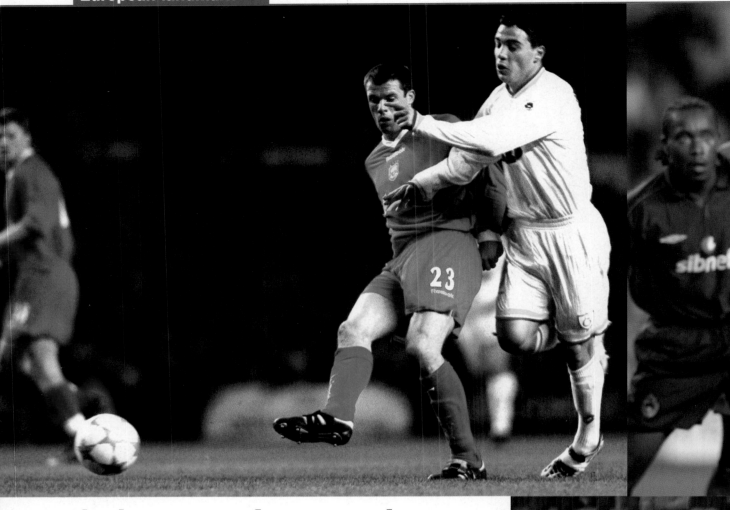

Homing in on Cally's Euro record

Carra in action against (clockwise from top left) Galatasaray, CSKA Moscow, Real Betis and Juventus

I T is safe to say that Jamie Carragher is unlikely to trouble Ian Rush at the top of the list of Liverpool's all-time leading goalscorers.

Nor is he likely to surpass Ian Callaghan's tally of 857 appearances in a Reds shirt.

But one honour Carra has set his sights on is the club's European appearance record. And if all goes to plan in this year's Champions League campaign he could well finish the season as the man who has represented the Reds in Europe more times than anyone else.

His most recent appearance in the final Champions League Group C match against Galatasaray on December 5 moved him into joint-second place with Tommy Smith on 85 appearances.

It means that if JC steers clear of injury and suspension and the Reds successfully come through their second round clash with Barcelona, he will equal Callaghan's total on April 10/11, 2007 in the quarter-final second leg.

"Oh I'd love to break it," said Carra.

"I'm not going to break any goal records, so it's down to the appearance records!

MOST EUROPEAN APPEARANCES FOR LIVERPOOL		
1	Ian Callaghan	89
2	Jamie Carragher	85
2=	Tommy Smith	85
4	Sami Hyypia	80
5	Ray Clemence	80
6	Emlyn Hughes	79
7	Phil Neal	74
8	Steven Gerrard	72
9	Steve Heighway	67
10	Chris Lawler	66

* Before February 2007

Season-by-season breakdown of European appearances	
1996/97	0
1997/98	1
1998/99	6
1999/00	0
2000/01	12
2001/02	16
2002/03	11
2003/04	4
2004/05	15
2005/06	13
2006/07	7

COMPETITION	GAMES	GOALS
C League	55	1
UEFA Cup	28	-
Super Cup	2	-

"We're fortunate now. With the Champions League you play a lot more games and I'm sure if they had had that in their day (Callaghan's) they would have played a lot more as well.

"But it would be nice to break it this season."

Carra's love affair with European competition began in the Cup Winners' Cup during the 1996/97 season.

The 19-year-old was an unused substitute in the second leg of a semi-final clash with Paris St Germain.

He may not have played in that match, but having witnessed the atmosphere of a big European night at Anfield from the bench he was eager to make an impact on the pitch.

The following season he got his chance when he started in a UEFA Cup first round match against Celtic on September 30, 1997.

It was the only appearance he made in the competition that season but it began an impressive run that has seen him feature in Europe in no fewer than nine of the 11 seasons he has been a member of the first team squad, collecting a UEFA Cup and Champions League winners medal on the way.

Showing the world what he can do

... when he gets the chance

DURING the summer of 2006 Jamie Carragher was belatedly given the opportunity to showcase his defensive qualities on the world stage – seven years after his international debut.

The linchpin at the heart of the Reds defence featured in four of England's five World Cup matches after missing out on the 2002 finals in Japan/South Korea through injury.

It was the first major tournament he had appeared in after being an unused substitute at Euro 2004.

His performances at right-back, in place of the injured Gary Neville, not only highlighted his versatility and ability to play across the back four but also proved once more, that at international level he is not regarded as one of England's first-choice defenders but more of a utility player.

While he has been one of the first names on the Liverpool teamsheet under both Gerard Houllier and Rafa Benitez he has failed to shake off the tag of 'reliable squad player' ever since he made his full debut under Kevin Keegan against Hungary in a 1-1 draw in Budapest on April 28, 1999.

Despite the honour of captaining the U21s and sharing the record for the most number of caps with Aston Villa's Gareth Barry, the statistic of just 14 starts from 31 full caps shows how Jamie's defensive qualities have yet to be fully appreciated at senior level.

No matter how well he performs for his beloved Reds he remains behind Rio Ferdinand and Ledley King in the pecking order to partner John Terry at the heart of England's defence.

Whether you agree with this or not it has restricted Carra to bit-part roles on the international scene, so much so that he did not make his competitive debut for England until September 2005.

His England career has been full of highs and lows and he even had the honour of captaining his country when he was one of four players to wear the armband during a friendly with Serbia & Montenegro on June 3, 2003.

However, such a proud moment has been dampened by the FA, who refuse to recognise Carra as having officially captained his country because he was not the skipper at the start of the match.

His most recent appearances for England have ended on a sour note after he missed a penalty in the World Cup Quarter-final shoot-out defeat to Portugal and in his last appearance for his country he was part of an experimental back three which proved unsuccessful in a Euro 2008 Qualifying defeat in Croatia.

ENGLAND

Carra's England stats

31 appearances
14 starts
 3 yellow cards

P	W	D	L
31	17	7	7

England U21s

Before the joy of signing his first professional contract with Liverpool or the realisaton of his dream to make an impact on the Reds' first team, Jamie Carragher made his debut for the England Under-21s.

Recognised for his leadership qualities, Carra was predominantly used as a holding midfielder and was later installed as the side's captain by manager Peter Taylor.

He led the side for the first time in a 4-1 win against Denmark.

Between 1996 and 2000 he was a mainstay in the side and established a record caps total in a 1-0 win over Argentina at Craven Cottage on February 22, 2000.

He went on to clock up 27 caps and still holds the record now alongside Aston Villa midfielder Gareth Barry.

Despite representing the Under-21s for over four years Carra only managed one goal, which came in a 2-0 win over Sweden in a European Under-21 Championship qualifying match on September 4, 1998.

MOST ENGLAND Under-21 appearances
Top 5

JAMIE CARRAGHER	27
Gareth Barry	27
David Prutton	25
Jermaine Pennant	24
Jermain Defoe	23

What he said and what they said about Carra's England career

"He rarely gets as much recognition as he deserves, but we know his qualities here.

"He is useful in many different positions and that's why I think England should take him to Euro 2004.

"I don't want to put pressure on Sven Goran Eriksson because I know how difficult his job is. But Carra can play left-back, right-back, centre-half and centre-midfield - and you need players in the squad that are versatile."

- Gerard Houllier's message to England boss Sven Goran Eriksson is clear about who he should take to Euro 2004.

"Jamie Carragher is an all-round player.

"He's played at centre-back for Liverpool all season, but he has played right-back, left-back and sitting midfielder in the past. He can do everything very well.

"I'm happy with him."

- Svan Goran Eriksson on CARRA (May 2006).

"When you think he is perceived to be fifth England centre-half behind Ledley King, John Terry, Rio and Sol then we must be the most blessed country in the world for defenders."

- Michael Owen, then at Real Madrid, praises CARRA's abilities in May 2005.

"I've never really had a decent run for England. There are a lot of good players who play ahead of me.

"If I ever get a run in the future, I'm sure I'll do a lot better as I've never really grabbed my England career with both hands or done as well as I've done for Liverpool."

- CARRA on his England career (September 2005).

"You don't get too many chances to play for England unless you're a superstar. There are certain players who you know are going to play because they're that good, and I'm not one of them."

- CARRA assesses his England hopes with typical honesty.

"It's not like at Liverpool if you go out of the FA Cup and the Champions League and there is always next year. This only comes around every four years and this makes it even tougher to take."

- CARRA on England's penalty shoot-out exit

Carra faces the twin pressure of having to score a penalty in a World Cup quarter-final and seeing Garth Crooks staring at him while (right) he helps Peter Crouch enjoy a goal against Uruguay

to Portugal in the 2006 World Cup quarter-finals.

"I think we have the nucleus of a top team, and you look in two years' time at the Euros and to the World Cup and see hope. We have got Theo Walcott and Aaron Lennon coming through. You look at the impact Lennon has made when he has come on in the games and

realise he has got great potential."

- CARRA on England's future - post Germany 2006.

"The referee said he never blew his whistle so I had to wait until after he blew it. I didn't realise. I obviously don't take that many. I've taken two in my career and scored two before this one."

- CARRA on his missed penalty in the shoot-

FULL DEBUT

Friendly April 28, 1999
Drew 1-1 v Hungary (A)
Nepstadion, Budapest

TEAM: Seaman, Brown (Gray 73), P. Neville, Batty, Keown, Ferdinand (CARRAGHER 61), Sherwood, Shearer, Butt, Phillips (Heskey 82), McManaman (Redknapp)

Alan Shearer's first-half penalty is cancelled out by Hungarian full-back Janos Hrutka's goal 14 minutes from time.

FIRST START

Friendly August 15, 2001
Lost 0-2 v Holland (H)
White Hart Lane

TEAM: Martyn (James 46 (Wright 49)), G. Neville (Mills 46), Ashley Cole (Powell 46), CARRAGHER, Keown (Southgate 46), Brown (Ehiogu 49), Beckham (Carrick 46), Scholes (Owen 46), Andy Cole (Smith 69), Fowler (Barmby 46), Hargreaves (Lampard 46)

A first start but that was as good as it got for Carra as Sven Goran Eriksson's side were handed a harsh football lesson by a fluid Dutch side. Carra was the only England man to remain on the field throughout as Sven made history by fielding eleven substitutes.
Carra's night was soured by a 44th minute booking.

FIRST COMPETITIVE START

World Cup qualifier September 3, 2005
Won 1-0 v Wales (A)
Millennium Stadium

TEAM: Robinson, Young, A. Cole, CARRAGHER, Ferdinand, Wright-Phillips (Defoe 67), Beckham, Gerrard (Richardson 84), J. Cole, (Hargreaves 76), Lampard, Rooney

A long overdue first competitive start is his reward for a series of inspirational displays during Liverpool's magnificent Champions League campaign.
Partnering Rio Ferdinand at the heart of the England defence in the World Cup qualifier, Carra produces a solid display as England run out winners courtesy of Joe Cole's second-half strike.

out – the referee made him re-take the kick after he had scored from his first attempt.

"I'd like to think I have put down a marker for the future.

"There is a game on Wednesday now and hopefully my performance can get me in the team for that match.
- CARRA sets his sights on a regular England place after a strong display in the 1-0 win over

Wales at the Millennium Stadium in 2005.

"To have lost in that manner and to have come on at half-time was the worst thing about it for me. It doesn't look good on your CV. For the ones who went off in Copenhagen, it was the best half they have ever had!"
- CARRA reflects on the 4-1 hammering in a friendly in Denmark in August 2005.

AN inauspicious start to the Reds' 2005/06 Premiership campaign brought Rafa Benitez's men crashing back down to earth following the euphoria of Istanbul.

A 2-0 defeat at Fulham on October 22 left the Reds languishing in the bottom half of the league table and was followed by a shock exit in the Carling Cup against Championship side Crystal Palace three days later.

With pressure mounting, Benitez urged his side to rediscover their form and put together a run of results to save their season.

The Reds responded in magnificent fashion and sandwiched between a superb 18-match unbeaten run they established a new club record of eleven consecutive clean sheets.

The men responsible for securing their place in history as 'Liverpool's shut-out kings' inevitably included Carra alongside Pepe Reina in his debut season, Sami Hyypia, Steve Finnan and John Arne Riise.

Thou shalt not pass

The 11 clean sheets that made history

WEST HAM Premiership (H)
Won 2-0, 29/10/05
Following the Carling Cup exit at Selhurst Park the Reds got back to winning ways with a 2-0 win over the Hammers.
ATTACKERS: David Bellion & Marlon Harewood

ANDERLECHT Champs League (H)
Won 3-0, 01/11/05
Another comfortable triumph was underlined by a sublime headed goal by Luis Garcia in front of the Kop.
The Belgians' miserable run of straight defeats in the competition rose to 11 with dangerman Mpenza limited to half-chances.
ATTACKERS: Mbo Mpenza & Akin Serhat

ASTON VILLA Premiership (A)
Won 2-0, 05/11/05
A cagey contest came to life in the final 10 minutes with goals from Steven Gerrard (pen) and Xabi Alonso giving the Reds their first back-to-back victories in the league.
Czech striker Baros failed to impress against his former club and was well marshalled by Carra.
ATTACKERS: Milan Baros & Kevin Phillips

Carra in action against Sao Paulo, shutting out former team-mate Milan Baros in the 2-0 win at Villa (left) and with centre-back partner Sami Hyypia

PORTSMOUTH Premiership (H)
Won 3-0, 19/11/05
Alain Perrin's side were swept aside as the Reds continued their winning run. The visitors struggled to seriously trouble the back four with Lua Lua starved of service.
ATTACKERS: Lomana Lua Lua & substitute Collins Mbesuma

REAL BETIS Champs League (H)
Drew 0-0, 23/11/05
Progression to the Last 16 was confirmed despite the frustration of missing a catalogue of chances against the side from Seville. Carra & co saw off a late Betis charge to maintain the run of shut-outs.
ATTACKERS: Xisco & Joaquin

MAN CITY Premiership (A)
Won 1-0, 26/11/05
Another three points were secured courtesy of Riise's second-half drive. Shot-shy City had just one shot on target as Liverpool cruised.
ATTACKERS: Darius Vassell & Andy Cole

SUNDERLAND Premiership (A)
Won 2-0, 30/11/05
Liverpool won their re-arranged match at a canter to condemn the Wearsiders to their seventh straight league defeat. The run of clean sheets was barely threatened as Jonathan Stead endured another joyless evening against one of the Premiership's meanest defences.
ATTACKER: Jonathan Stead

WIGAN Premiership (H)
Won 3-0, 03/12/05
The match went down in history for being the game in which Peter Crouch broke his scoring duck with his first and second in 19 games.
The supposed threat of the Latics' pacy strike-force failed to materialise as a first-half goal-fest left Paul Jewell's men well beaten at Anfield.
ATTACKERS: Jason Roberts & Henri Camara

CHELSEA Champs League (A)
Drew 0-0, 06/12/05
An impressive display saw the Reds contain the Premiership leaders comfortably with Carra once more superb at the back.
The home side pressed late on but just like in the previous season's Champions League matches they could not break through Liverpool's dogged resistance.
ATTACKERS: Didier Drogba & Eidur Gudjohnsen

MIDDLESBROUGH Premiership (H)
Won 2-0, 10/12/05
Rafa Benitez's men were frustrated for large parts of this match until a late Fernando Morientes double secured the points.
It meant Reina had not conceded a goal in over 10 hours of football.
ATTACKERS: Mark Viduka & Yakubu

DEPORTIVO SAPRISSA World Club Championship (N), Won 3-0, 15/12/05
The Reds eased into the final of the World Club Championship with a simple win over the Costa Ricans that saw the Reds establish their clean sheet record.
ATTACKERS: Alvaro Soborio & Ronald Gomez

All good things come to an end...

SAO PAULO World Club Championship (N)
Lost 1-0, 18/12/05
Despite dominating throughout and having three goals ruled out for offside the Reds slumped to defeat and conceded their first goal in over 17 hours of football when Mineiro ran clear to place the ball past Reina.
ATTACKERS: Amoroso & Aloisio